NEBRASKA: OUR PIONEER HERITAGE

by
Dr. Robert N. Manley

Lincoln, Nebraska

Library of Congress Catalog Card No. 81 — 80750
ISBN 0-939644-00-2

Illustrations by Eric Warp

Cover Design and Art by Chuck Elley

First edition — First printing

Printed in United States of America

**For Joy and Becky
and all of Nebraska's
children**

Table of Contents

DR. ROBERT MANLEY

Hello, boys and girls. I want to talk with you for just a minute about this book I've written for you.

First of all, this is a book about Nebraska. I wrote the book especially for you students who live in Nebraska.

As you read my book I know you will discover that Nebraska has an exciting past. You will also find that Nebraska's history is the story of people — people just like you and me.

And you will find that there is history in every part of Nebraska. In every town and city, on every farm and ranch in our State, there is history just waiting to be discovered.

Don't be surprised if some of the best stories you find are about people in your own family. Your family is a part of history too.

Remember this: History is the story of people, all kinds of people. And history is around you no matter where you live in Nebraska.

I hope you enjoy reading my book. I know you will have fun as you learn about Nebraska, the State where we live.

The title of this book is

NEBRASKA: OUR PIONEER HERITAGE

Now I want to ask you a question: what is a pioneer?

Last year I asked a class of Nebraska students that question. Timmy was the first to raise his hand.

"Dr. Manley, pioneers were men and women who came to Nebraska many years ago. They were the first settlers in Nebraska."

Kim thought for a moment and then she said, "The explorers and fur traders were pioneers, weren't they?"

"What about the soldiers who lived in the Army posts along the trails?" asked Becky. "They were pioneers too."

Joy raised her hand. "The farmers who plowed the sod and planted the first crops were Nebraska pioneers. I'm sure of that!"

I could tell that Angie had some other pioneers in mind. I asked her to tell us who she was thinking about.

"Well," she said slowly, "I think the men and women who built towns in Nebraska were pioneers."

Then Johnnie called out from the back of the room. He was so excited he didn't even raise his hand before he spoke.

"I know one group of pioneers we shouldn't forget!" Johnnie said loudly. "How about the cowboys? They were real Nebraska pioneers!"

I thought the students had some good answers for my question. They told me about some interesting Nebraska pioneers.

Can you think of some pioneers they didn't tell me about? What other Nebraska pioneers can you think of?

Now I want to ask **you** a question.
Why were the Nebraska pioneers important?
Pioneers were important because they prepared the way for those of us who live in Nebraska today.
A pioneer is a person who prepares the way for others.

Pioneers drove their covered wagons across the land. Our highways follow the trails the pioneers made.

Pioneers built the towns and cities where we live.

They plowed the land and made farms. Many Nebraskans live on farms that were made by their pioneer ancestors.

Then there were the pioneer cattlemen of western Nebraska. Today fat cattle graze on the rich Nebraska grass. Years ago cowboys herded Texas longhorns on this range land.

These are some of the ways the pioneers prepared the way for us.

And do you know what? Each one of us can be a pioneer. That's right!

Just as the first Nebraska pioneers prepared the way for us, we can prepare the way for *our* children and grandchildren.

Can you think of some things you might do to prepare the way for your children?

Perhaps one of you will invent a new kind of fuel to be used in our cars. That would be great, wouldn't it? Or one of you might discover a new way of raising crops. That would also be great. And maybe one of you will invent a new kind of rocket that your children can ride in as they fly to outer space. Wouldn't that be exciting?

What kind of pioneer would you like to be?

Now that you understand the word *pioneer* we can get started. This book is going to tell you about some very special pioneers. You are going to learn about the pioneers who were the first settlers in Nebraska. And remember: these Nebraska pioneers prepared the way for us!

Some Interesting Nebraska Pioneers!

Women Track Stars!
University of Nebraska, 1903

UNIT ONE: ON YOUR MARK!

In this first unit you will meet a Nebraska pioneer with an unusual name.

You will also learn about Nebraska, the land of the pioneers.

Chapter One:
The Story of Billy Bugeater

The year is 1875. You and I are standing at the railroad depot in Omaha. The people around us are very excited. They see the train coming down the track.

As the train pulls into the station, the engine whistle gives a shrill blast. Clouds of steam and smoke hiss loudly from the big engine. The cars stop with a jerk. Men, women and children quickly climb down from the cars.

See the man who just got off the train? He is a newspaper reporter from New York City.

Why has he come to Nebraska?

His newspaper has sent him to write a story about Nebraska. People in the East have heard about the terrible drought in Nebraska. It hasn't rained for months, and most of the crops have dried up and died.

The New York Daily Times
Drought in Nebraska

And if that weren't bad enough, billions of grasshoppers have dropped from the sky. The terrible insects have chewed up every green plant.

The newspaper reporter has come to find out if the stories are true. So he travels around Nebraska. He talks to farmers and he finds that the stories are true. Crops in the fields have died. Trees and gardens have been picked clean by the grasshoppers.

The reporter sits down and writes an article for his newspaper. Here is part of what he wrote:

E NEW YORI

> In Nebraska the grasshoppers have eaten the corn. Chinch bugs have eaten the wheat. The potato bugs have eaten the potatoes. I fear the only thing left for the people to eat are the bugs.

We know that the reporter was just joking. Although life was hard in Nebraska, the people did not eat bugs. Men were able to get food for their families.

But folks in the East did not forget the story. They made jokes about Nebraska and the bugs. They said that only "bugeaters" could live in Nebraska.

At first the people who lived in Nebraska were angry. They didn't like to be called "bug-eaters."

In time, however, they became proud of the title. After all, a Nebraska "bugeater" was a person who lived through the hard pioneer years.

A "bug-eater" was a person who did not give up. A "bug-eater" fought the dry weather and the grasshoppers. He and his family stayed on the land.

Yes, the pioneer men and women of Nebraska were proud to be called "bugeaters."

A family of Nebraska "bugeaters."

I would like you to meet an imaginary friend of mine. His name is Billy Bugeater, and Billy has something to say to you.

"Hi, boys and girls. My name is Billy Bugeater. I lived in Nebraska back in pioneer days when life was not always easy."

"I've seen Nebraska grow and change. I've seen the people of Nebraska make wonderful farms and ranches on the land. I've seen them build prosperous towns. What I've seen makes me proud to be a Nebraska pioneer!"

"I want to help you learn about Nebraska — so you can be proud of our State, just as I am. Follow me and I'll tell you about Nebraska's pioneers — the men and women who prepared the way for you.

"We are going to have fun as we discover the exciting story of Nebraska's pioneers. O.K. Let's go!"

Chapter Two:
Nebraska: Land of the Pioneers

Nebraska is the name of the State where you and I live. Do you know what "Nebraska" means?

In the language of the Omaha Indians, "Nebraska" means "flat water." What do you suppose the Indians meant by "flat water"?

The Indians were probably describing the Platte River which flows all the way across Nebraska.

The Platte River is very wide and shallow. It looks like "flat water" as it flows across the land.

Look at this picture of the Platte River. It will help you understand why the Indians called it "flat water."

Nebraska, as you know, is one State in our country, the United States. Find the State of Nebraska on a map of our country.

Can you name the States which are around Nebraska?

How big is Nebraska? One way to find out is by comparing Nebraska with other States. Which is larger, Texas or Nebraska?

Is Massachusetts larger or smaller than Nebraska?
Is California or Nebraska the larger State?

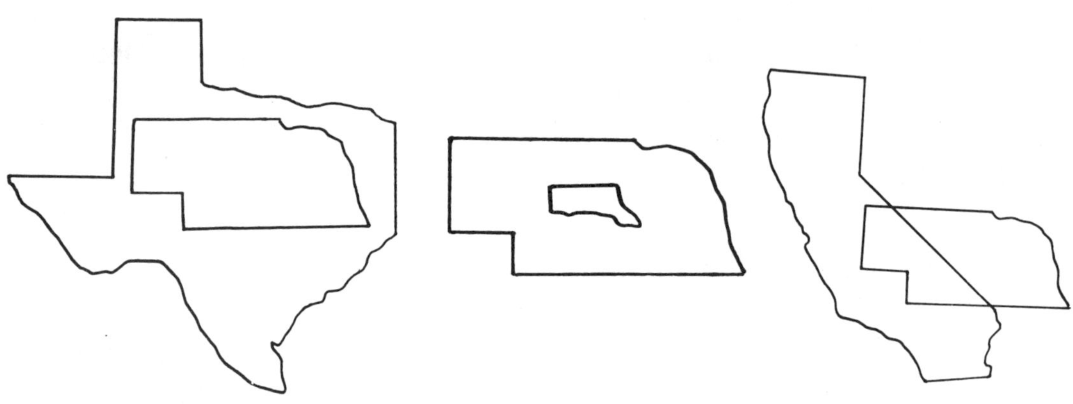

The map below shows the counties of Nebraska.
How many counties are there in Nebraska?

What is the name of the county where you live?
What other Nebraska counties have you and your classmates lived in?

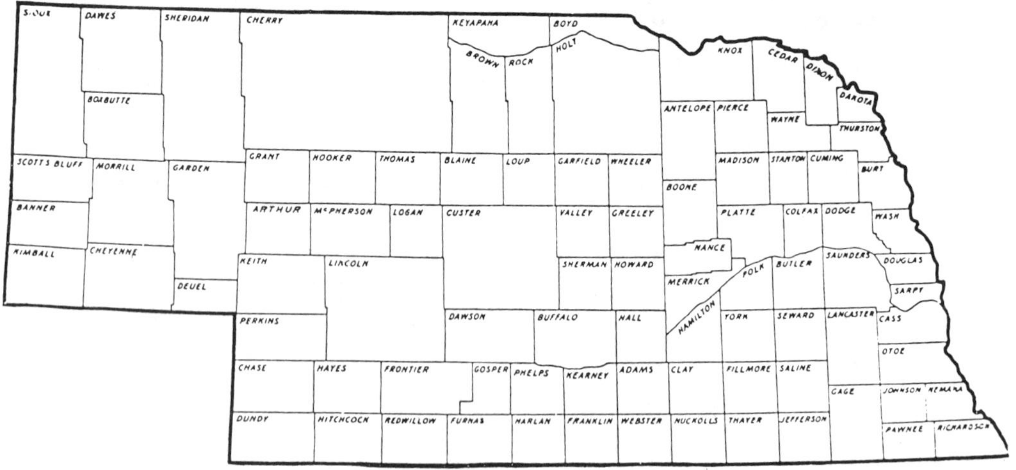

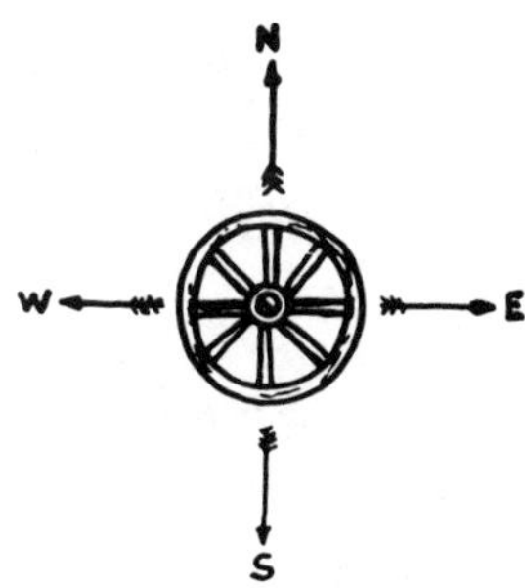

Get a large map of your county and put it on the wall.

1. How large is your county?
2. What is the county seat of your county?
3. What is the name of your county? How did your county get its name?

Here are some other questions for you to answer.

1. How far is a mile? Can you think of a place that is one mile from your school?
2. How many miles do you live from school?
3. How long does it take you to get to your school in a car?
4. If you had to walk to school, how long would the trip take you?

Next, study this map of Nebraska.

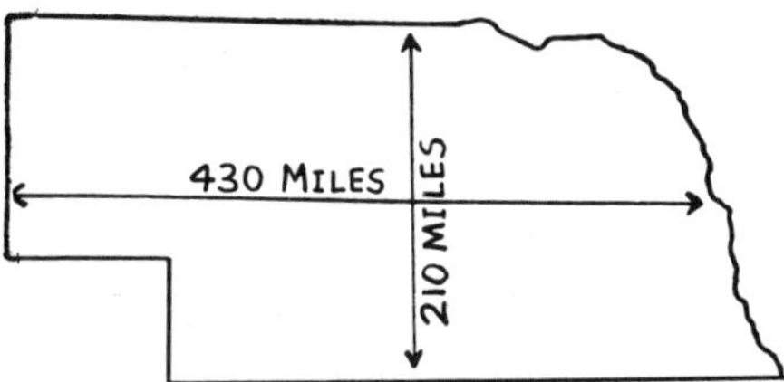

Can you tell directions on a map? (The figure at the left will help you find directions on the map.)

What direction on a map is north?

What direction on a map is south?

What direction on a map is east?

What direction on a map is west?

Here are some other questions about this map:

1. How far is it across Nebraska from east to west?
2. How far is it across Nebraska from south to north?

The map you see below tells us the distances between some Nebraska cities.

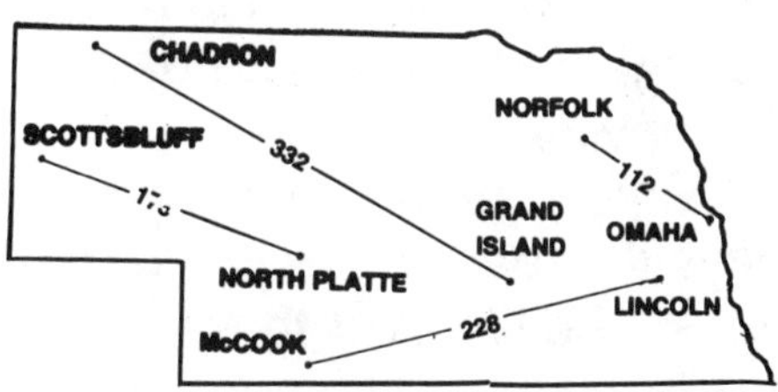

How far is it from Omaha to Norfolk?

How far is it from Lincoln to McCook?

How far is it from Chadron to Grand Island?

How far is it from Scottsbluff to North Platte?

Today you and your family can drive across Nebraska in your automobile in about nine hours.

A pioneer family traveling in a covered wagon drawn by oxen took three weeks to make the same trip. Think of that! Aren't you glad you are not living in pioneer days?

Suppose that a pioneer farmer who lived near Brownville needed to take a load of corn to Beatrice. How long would it take him to make the trip to Beatrice and back to Brownville?

Remember that in pioneer days the roads were just dirt trails. The trip over these bad roads would take the farmer almost a week.

Today we can drive a car from Brownville to Beatrice and back to Brownville in three hours.

A trip by car from Lincoln to McCook takes five hours. How long do you think it took a pioneer stagecoach to make the same trip?

A stagecoach, drawn by four horses, could make the trip in two days — but this meant some traveling after dark. And night travel in a stagecoach was very dangerous.

Automobiles go from Scottsbluff to North Platte in about four hours today.

Suppose you were a pioneer cowboy who worked on a ranch near Scottsbluff. You had business in North Platte. So you saddled up your best horse and started for North Platte. How long would the trip on horseback take you?

Depending upon the weather — and depending upon whether you ran into hostile Indians or robbers along the trail — the trip would take three or four days.

Pretend you have just arrived in Grand Island, Nebraska. You have come from New York State to look for good farm land. In Grand Island you hear about some land near Chadron. You decide to go to Chadron and look at the land.

You have one problem. You don't have any money. There is only one way for you to get to Chadron. You must walk.

How long would it take a pioneer to walk from Grand Island to Chadron? If the pioneer didn't get lost, he could make it in about two weeks.

Today, in our automobiles, we can make the trip in six or seven hours.

Let's pretend you know a man who lives in Falls City. He needs to go to Omaha on business. Back in the 1850's, during pioneer days, the easiest way to get to Omaha was by steamboat on the Missouri River. How long would the steamboat trip take?

It would take a steamboat two days to make the trip. Today we drive the same distance in two hours.

Finally, a family in Omaha wants to visit some friends in Norfolk. The year is 1880 and they know they can go by steam railroad to Norfolk. How long would it take the steam train to make the trip?

The family would bounce around in the train for ten hours before they arrived in Norfolk.

We can drive between the two cities in two or three hours today.

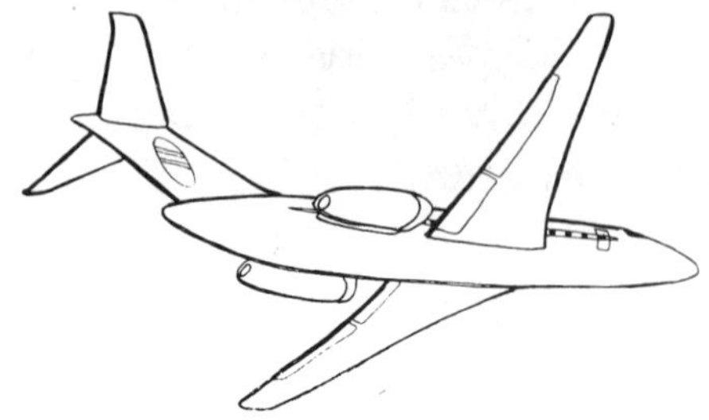

Wouldn't the pioneers be amazed by how fast we travel today?

I'm sure no pioneer would believe that today we can cross Nebraska by jet airplane in less than an hour!

To the pioneers, with their slow and difficult ways of traveling, Nebraska must have seemed like a very big State.

Nebraska is the State where we live! **Nebraska** means "flat water."

The pioneers thought Nebraska was a very big State. Pioneers usually traveled by wagon. Now jet airplanes fly over Nebraska!

Nebraska is the land of the Pioneers.

UNIT TWO: HISTORY & HERITAGE

Chapter 3:
History and Heritage

Please think about the word "history" for a minute. What does the word "history" mean to you?

Listen as some students tell us what the word "history" means to them.

Those are very good answers. History does tell us about the past. History also tells us about famous people and important events that happened in the past.

But history is something else.
Listen to our friend, Billy Bug-eater:

HISTORY IS THE STORY OF PEOPLE

The first thing you should know about history is that it is the story of people, all kinds of people. This means that history includes the story of you and your family.

You must not think that history is the story of other people. Don't be like these students.

Sorry to say, I find that many students believe that nothing important ever happened to the members of their family.

But they are wrong!

As students learn about their families, they discover interesting, exciting history right in their own families.

Students discover they have family stories like this one:

This is a small village in central Europe. It is thousands of miles from this village to Nebraska. The year is 1879.

In one of the houses a family sits down to eat their supper. Father, mother and two children are seated at the table. (Let's pretend that this is your great grandfather's family.)

The father and mother are very tired. They have worked all day in the fields of their farm. There isn't much food on the table. They seem to be very discouraged.

The father speaks. (One thing to remember: your great grandfather would speak in a foreign language.)

"I'm afraid you children have no future in this land. Your life is going to be very hard. Every day you will go to work in the fields, just as I have done for my whole life."

The mother then speaks. "What shall we do, Papa? I want our children to go to school. I want them to have an education. I want our boy to own his own land. I want our girl to have a fine home. I want them to have a wonderful future!"

The father thinks for a moment. Then he says, "Mama, I think we should go to America."

The children jump up from their chairs. As they dance around the room they cry out, "Where is America? How do we get there? When do we leave?"

As you discover the story of your family, you are going to find many stories like this one. Exciting and important things happened to people in your family.

Listen very carefully: the part of history which tells the story of you and your family has a special name.

It is called your **HERITAGE.**

HERITAGE. That is a very important world. **HERITAGE** is your very own history. It is the story of you and your family.

As you study history in school, you find a part of your **HERITAGE** on just about every page of your history book.

An exciting way to study history is by discovering the story of your own family. You will find that you have had some very interesting **ancestors.** Who are your **ancestors?**

Your ancestors are the men and women who lived before you were born.

Among your ancestors you will find many pioneers. These pioneers are the people who prepared the way for you.

Who were important pioneers in your family? Can you tell the class about the men and women in your family who were pioneers?

Who is your favorite family pioneer?

"REMEMBER: HISTORY IS THE STORY OF PEOPLE. HERITAGE IS THE STORY OF YOU AND YOUR FAMILY."

"Start today to discover your family pioneers."

Time to Think and Talk

1. On a piece of paper write down your definition of "history." Put this paper away in a safe place. When you finish reading this book, take out this written definition. See if you can write a better definition of history.

2. What is "heritage"? Who do you study when you study "heritage"?

3. What does the word "ancestor" mean?

4. Make a list of some of your ancestors. Write down some interesting facts you have learned about these ancestors.

5. Who is your favorite family pioneer? Write a story about this family pioneer. Read this story to the class. Perhaps you would like to make some drawings to illustrate the story of your favorite family pioneer.

Nebraska's State Bird
is the meadowlark.

Chapter 4:
Looking for Your Heritage

"Heritage is your very own history. It is the story of you and your family."

Let's think of the ways we discover our heritage.

Is there someone in your family who is interested in **genealogy?** If there is, that person can help you discover the story of your family.

A person who is interested in **genealogy** studies the history of his or her family. A genealogist finds the names of every member of the family going back over many, many generations.

Perhaps someone has written a genealogy book about your family. If your family has such a book, you are really lucky. It will help you learn about your family.

Many of us don't know much about our genealogy. We don't have books written about our family.

But we can discover the story of our family in other ways—and we can have fun doing it.

First of all, you can look around your house for "pieces" of your heritage. What is a "piece" of heritage?

A "piece" of heritage is any thing that tells you about you and your family.

A piece of old furniture that belonged to one of your ancestors is an interesting "piece" of heritage.

Old letters written by someone in your family are really valuable "pieces" of heritage.

A trunk filled with clothing that people in your family used to wear contains many interesting "pieces" of heritage.

Look through the boxes that are stored in the basement of your house for "pieces" of your heritage. Dig into closets and drawers. Keep looking and you will find exciting "pieces" of heritage that tell you about you and your family.

Old family photographs are just about the most exciting "pieces" of heritage you can find. Family photographs are very important. Photographs show you what your ancestors looked like. They show you how they lived and how they dressed.

As you discover family photographs study them closely. Ask your parents to help you answer questions about the family photograph:

1. Who are the people in the photograph?
2. Where was the photograph taken?
3. When was the photograph taken?
4. Why was the photograph taken?

As you get answers for these questions, the family photograph becomes very important piece of your heritage.

Just for practice, look at the photographs on the next page. See if you can think up answers for the four questions.

"Photographs help you discover your heritage. Find some old family photographs. Learn all you can about the people in the photographs."

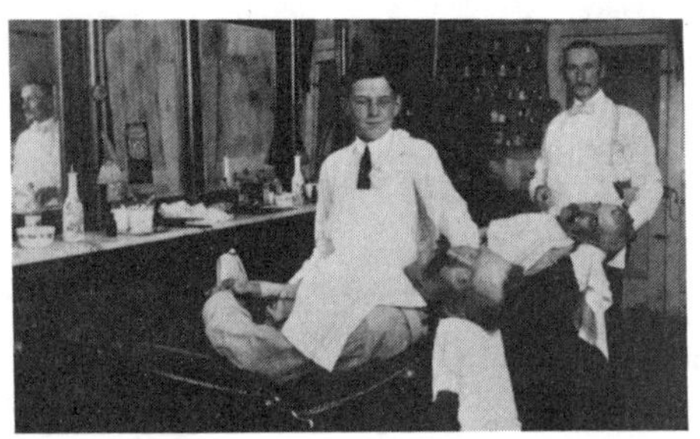

Heritage in a cemetery

A metal star by a gravestone or a star carved on the marker means that the man served in the Union Army during the Civil War. The letters GAR stand for the Grand Army of the Republic. This was the organization to which Union Army veterans belonged. The dates, 1861-1865, are the years of the Civil War.

We know that the person buried here is of Czech descent. The letters ZCBJ stand for a Czech lodge, or club, to which the person belonged.

Buried here is a man who belonged to the Odd Fellows Lodge. The links of chain are the sign of the lodge. The letters stand for Friendship, Love and Truth. Lodges were very important. People had good times at lodge meetings. The lodges also provided insurance for the men and provided homes for windows and orphans of the members.

Chapter 5:
Listening For Your Heritage

You can discover your heritage by listening.

All of us have had wonderful listening experiences. There was the time we listened to our grandfather tell about his first automobile. Or the time one of our aunts talked about going to school back "in the good old days."

Yes, we can learn about our heritage by listening to our parents, grandparents and other adults.

What are some good ways we can learn by listening?

One way is by asking your parents to answer some questions. Say to your parents, "Dad and Mom, I want to learn about what you were doing when you were my age. Would you answer some questions for me, please?"

Here are some questions to ask your mother and father:

1. When you were my age, where were you living?
2. Tell me about your family. How many brothers and sisters did you have?
3. When you were my age, what did you and your brothers and sisters do for fun?
4. Tell me about your father and mother.
5. What kind of work did your father do?
6. What is something special you remember about your mother?
7. Who were your best friends? Why did you like them?
8. Tell me about your school. What was it like?
9. Do you remember any of your teachers? What were your teachers like? Who was your favorite teacher?
10. What did you like about school?

11. What did you do for fun when you were my age?
12. Do you remember the best time you had with your family? What did you do?
13. Who was your favorite relative? Tell me about your favorite relative.
14. Did you ever get into trouble with your parents? If you don't mind, please tell me about that time.
15. When you were my age, did you ever think about what you wanted to be when you grew up? What did you think you wanted to be when you grew up?

After listening to your parents answer these questions—and any other questions you can think of—you will know some interesting things about your parents.

Here is a good idea! Why not ask your grandparents the same questions? And there may be other members of your family, such as aunts and uncles, you can listen to also.

It is fun listening to people talk about the past.

"It is fun listening to stories about your family. This is a good way to discover your heritage!"

I'm sure you will find that there are many adults you will want to listen to. Some will be members of your family. Others may be interesting men and women in your town or your neighborhood.

Why don't you set up a **PEOPLE BANK?**

What is a **PEOPLE BANK?**

A **PEOPLE BANK** is a place where you keep the names of men and women you want to talk with. It can be a sheet of paper in your notebook. It can be a box on your desk. Or it can be a bulletin board in your classroom.

You put the names of people in this **PEOPLE BANK;** and as you have time, you go to talk to them.

You will probably put many, many names in your **PEOPLE BANK.** It may take you a long time to talk to all of them. But that is all right. Don't be in a hurry.

Some of the people you may want to visit several times. All of the people you listen to will become your good friends.

It is fun to listen to men and women tell about the past. They can tell you about your heritage and about the pioneers who prepared the way for you.

"Listening...is a great way to discover the story of you and your family."

The people in your **PEOPLE BANK** will help you understand that you and your family are a part of history.

And do you know what? Some day **your** children will want to know about you! They will want to know what you were doing when you were their age.

Don't you think it would be a good idea for you to put some pieces of your heritage away for your children and grandchildren to have? These pieces of heritage would tell them about you.

Here is one thing you can do. Take a piece of paper and write the story of you. Write down what you are doing right now in school,at home. After you have finished your story, seal it in an envelop and put it in a safe place. Some day your children and grandchildren will enjoy reading the story you have written.

Here is another good idea. Get a tape recorder and make a tape of your answers to the questions you asked your parents. Then, have your friends answer the same questions. Save these tapes and put them away in a safe place.

Won't your children be excited when they hear you talking about yourself? Won't they enjoy listening to your friends talk about school?

Your written stories and the tape cassettes will help your children and grandchildren know that they have a past. They will know that they have a wonderful heritage.

"It is very important for you to save some pieces of your heritage for your children."

HERITAGE SPECIAL

The story of your family name.

Did you know that there is history in your family name?

Many hundreds of years ago one of your ancestors decided to name his family.

For example, my name is Manley. That means that my ancestor lived in the town of Manley in Cheshire, England.

My mother's family name was Cameron. This meant that the family lived near Cameron, which meant Crooked Hill, in Scotland. It also meant that the man who had the name had a crooked nose. How about that?

Here are just a few interesting family name histories for you to read:

Fisher—an English name meaning that the man caught fish.

Keller—a German name which meant that the man worked in a storeroom.

Kuhl—a German name meaning that the family lived along a stream or river.

Smith—an English name for a man who worked as a blacksmith.

Schmidt—a German name for a man who worked as a blacksmith.

Miller—a German or English name meaning that the man worked in a flour mill.

Jonsson—a Swedish name which meant that the man was "the son of John."

Ackerman—a German or English name which tells us that the man took care of the plow horses.

Farinella—an Italian name adopted by the man who carried flour from the flour mill to the houses in the village.

Bailey—an English name taken by the man who worked for a king or lord and who looked after his master's property and lands.

Isn't that interesting? See if you can discover the story of your family name. It will tell you something interesting about your heritage.

Ask your teacher to get this book from the library: E. C. Smith, *The New Dictionary of American Family Names.* This book will help you discover the story of your family name.

UNIT THREE LISTEN TO THE LAND

These boys and girls are learning to "listen to the land."

In this Unit you will learn how you can "listen to the land."

Chapter 6:
Voices From the Past

My family and I lived for a time in McCook. I had a good friend in McCook. His name was John, and he was a retired farmer.

One day I asked John if he knew anything about the history of the land around McCook.

"You bet I do," John replied. "My grandparents were pioneers in Red Willow County. I can tell you many stories about the people who settled this land."

So I asked John to share some of his stories with me. And I asked him if he would show me the country.

We climbed into his old pick-up truck and drove off into the country.

Suddenly, John stopped the car. "Let's get out," he said to me. "I want to show you something."

We left the car and climbed through a tangled barbed wire fence along the road. We walked up to an old, abandoned farm house.

"My grandfather built this house," John told me. "My family lived in this old house for many, many years. In fact, I was born in that house."

John then said, "Follow me, Bob." John walked away from the house and started down the hill behind the house. When we got to the bottom of the hill he stopped. He pointed to a hole in the side of the hill.

"You know what that is?" he asked.

I shook my head. It just looked like a big hole in the ground to me.

"Well, that is what is left of the dugout my grandfather made for his family when they first came to this land. That was long before I was born, but I remember my grandfather telling some interesting stories about life in that dugout."

As John and I drove back to town, he shared with me many stories about his family. He told me about the hard times they had faced—years of drought and hard times. But he also told me about the many good times they had enjoyed.

I asked him how he remembered all those wonderful stories.

John thought for a moment. Then he said, "I guess I've just learned to listen to the land."

What do you suppose John meant? How can you "listen to the land"? The land can't talk, can it?

Of course the land can't talk. But you and I can find wonderful people in Nebraska who can tell us about the land and the pioneers who lived on the land.

You can listen to these exciting stories. Then when you travel over Nebraska, you will remember the stories of the pioneers you have heard. Then you can "listen to the land."

As you "listen to the land," you will discover something very important. You will find that no matter where you live in Nebraska, you will find people who can tell you about the pioneers and the land.

You will learn about Nebraska from books. But you will also learn about our State by talking to old-timers, like my friend John.

So, get busy with your People Bank. Find the men and women who live in your community who can help you "listen to the land."

HERITAGE SPECIAL

Names on the Land.

An interesting way to discover the story of the land is by learning about the names which we find on the land. Here are some examples:

Hoosier Valley is in Stanton County. Hoosiers are people from Indiana. So we know that pioneers from Indiana settled in this valley.

Stinking Water Creek. That is an interesting name, isn't it? Buffalo would get stuck in the muddy creek and die. Their bodies then would rot and give off a bad odor.

Breakneck Hill. There are several hills with this name in Nebraska. A steep road ran down the hills. Any pioneer in a wagon or stagecoach who went down the road too fast ran the risk of breaking his neck.

Yankee Hill, near Lincoln, is where a group of Yankees settled. Yankees are pioneers who came from New England.

Dane Creek is near Ord in Valley County. Pioneers from Denmark lived along the Creek.

Bloody Run is a small stream in Sherman County. One story is that two men who lived along the creek got into a fight. In their struggle they fell into the creek. After their fierce fight, blood ran down the stream.

Look around where you live. See what interesting names on the land you can find.

Ask your teacher if you can set up a bulletin board in your classroom on which you can put the interesting names you find.

There are wonderful stories to be found in the names on your land.

Chapter 7:
A Look At Our Land

Right now I want you to pretend that it is a warm, bright June day. We are standing at the Omaha airport. We have rented an airplane and we are going to fly across Nebraska. Sounds like fun, doesn't it? There is no better way to look at our land.

Here comes our pilot. "Hi, everybody," he calls out. "Ready for our trip?"

"Yes! Yes!" we all yell. "Let's go!"

"Before we take off," says the pilot, "let me show you where we are going."

He spreads a map out on the wing of the airplane for us to see.

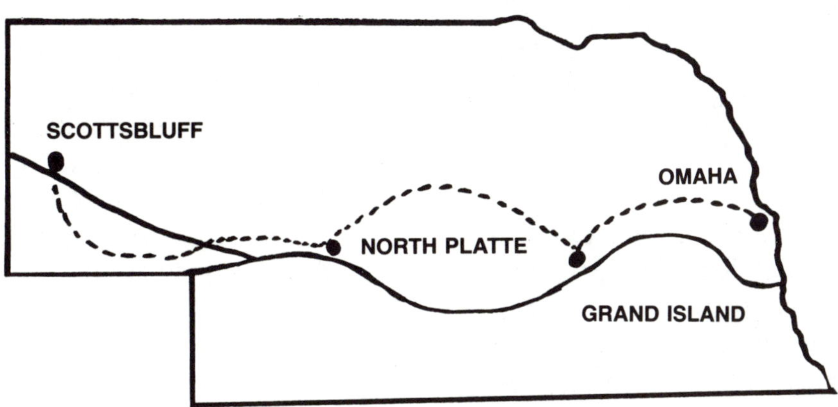

"We are going to fly from Omaha to Scottsbluff. See that dotted line? That is the course we are going to follow. Our trip will give you a good chance to look at the land."

We climb into the plane. A few minutes later we roar down the runway and climb swiftly into the blue sky.

Look below! See the Missouri River? That muddy river has played an important role in the history of Nebraska.

The plane turns to the west, and we see the city of Omaha spread out beneath us. See the tall buildings and the wide ribbons of interstate highways!

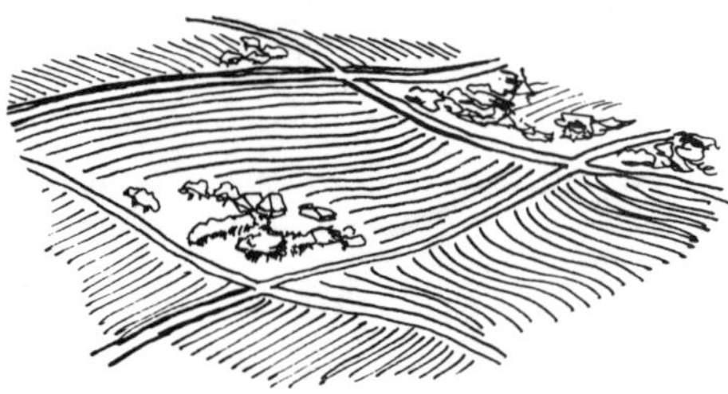

In just a few minutes Omaha is left behind. Now we are flying over rolling green hills. There are many trees. There are also many farms. Here and there we see a small town.

Look ahead! Do you see the broad Platte River? We can see now why the Indians called it "flat water."

Just think! Back in pioneer days thousands of covered wagons rolled along the Platte River. In a good day of travel the wagons went fifteen or twenty miles.

In our airplane we go twenty miles in about half a minute. Isn't that something?

Now we are passing over Grand Island. The pilot turns the airplane to the north. Soon we are over the Nebraska Sand Hills.

"Where is the sand?" someone asks. That is a good question. We don't see sand below us. No, we see miles and miles of grass-covered hills. There are many small lakes tucked between the hills. But, under the grass, the soil is very sandy. That is why they are called the Sand Hills.

This Sand Hills country is certainly different from eastern Nebraska. There aren't any small farms. Towns are very few. And there doesn't seem to be many trees, either.

We see herds of cattle grazing on the hills and around the lakes. We see ranches, and once in a while we spot a cowboy on his horse. He looks up and waves his hat as we fly over.

For a long time we fly over the Sand Hills. They look like the waves of a green ocean. This is some of the finest cattle country in the world.

Then the pilot points ahead. "Look over there!" he calls out. "Do you know what those bright green circles on the ground are?"

He swoops the plane down so we can get a close look.

We see that the green circles are fields of crops watered by center pivot irrigation systems.

All of us have seen those huge sprinklers that go around in a circle. They spread a fine spray of water on the thirsty crops.

Once again the pilot calls to us. "Up ahead is North Platte," he says.

By this time we've noticed another change in the land. The land now appears to be very rough and dry. Except where there are irrigated fields, the land looks brown. And there are very few farms on the land. Towns are few and far between too.

The pilot turns the plane southwest from North Platte. Once again the land seems to change. It is now flat and we see an amazing sight—we see wheat fields planted in long strips across the prairie. There is a strip of bright green wheat, then a strip of plowed ground, then another strip of wheat.

The wheat ranchers call this strip farming, and it is the way they raise wheat in western Nebraska.

The pilot banks our plane and we turn north. Up ahead we see the valley of the North Platte River. The land is rough and rugged. The prairie grass looks dry and brown.

"Look ahead," someone calls out. "There is Chimney Rock!"

Then we see Scott's Bluff and the city of Scottsbluff.

The pilot gently lands the plane on the concrete runway of the Scottsbluff airport.

We climb out of the airplane in front of the hangar. We look around. This certainly doesn't look like Omaha! Not at all!

One of the boys says, "Are you sure we are still in Nebraska?" We all laugh. And yet we all know what he means. The land in western Nebraska is so different from the land in the eastern part of our State.

Our airplane trip across Nebraska was fun, wasn't it? And we learned some important things.

First: We learned that Nebraska is a very big State. Even in an airplane, it took us a long time to fly across the State.

Second: We learned that there are many different parts to Nebraska. And each part of Nebraska looks different from the other parts of our State.

There are the green, tree lined hills of the Missouri River valley.

There are the small farms of eastern Nebraska, and the wide valley of the Platte River.

There is the huge cattle country we call the Sand Hills.

There are the irrigated farmlands of central Nebraska, and the large wheat ranches stretching across the prairie.

And there are the rugged, beautiful lands of western Nebraska.

We've discovered something very important about Nebraska. Our State is made up of many different kinds of land.

But one thing we also know: Nebraska is a very beautiful land. From East to West we saw a beautiful land.

Chapter 8:
Rain, Wind and Sun

In the last chapter we learned that Nebraska is made up of many different kinds of land.

Eastern Nebraska has many trees and rich, green, grass-covered hills.

In western Nebraska we saw a different land. There were few trees, and those we saw were different from the trees in the east. Even the western grass looked different.

Let's see if we can find out why the parts of Nebraska look so different.

First, let us pick up Nebraska from the map and turn the State on its side. Now look at Nebraska:

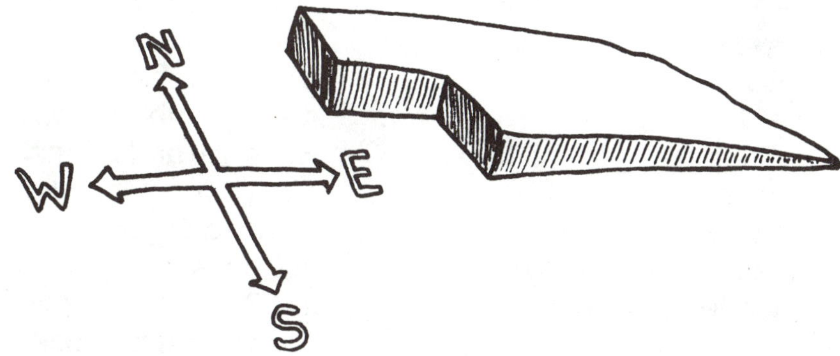

What does the map show us now?

It shows us that Nebraska runs uphill, from east to west. Do you see that?

A person in Scottsbluff is standing on land which is about 5,000 feet above sea level. At Omaha, a person is only 800 feet above the level of the sea.

So, as we travel across Nebraska on the land, going from east to west, we go steadily uphill.

Here is the important fact! As the land becomes higher it also becomes drier. Western Nebraska has much less rainfall than eastern Nebraska. That is one reason why the land, the trees and the grass change so much.

From the days of the pioneers, right up to our own time, weather has played a very important role in the history of Nebraska.

So, now let us talk about rain.

How many of you know what a rain gauge is? Here is a drawing of a rain gauge.

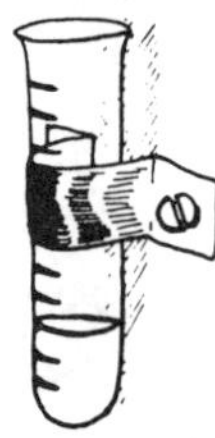

After a rain you can look at the gauge and tell how much rain fell. The container will hold the rainfall and tell you how much fell.

I'm sure you've heard your dad say, "We had an inch of rain last night." And TV weathermen are always talking about the amount of rain that fell in Nebraska.

Look at the map. This is what is known as a rainfall map of Nebraska.

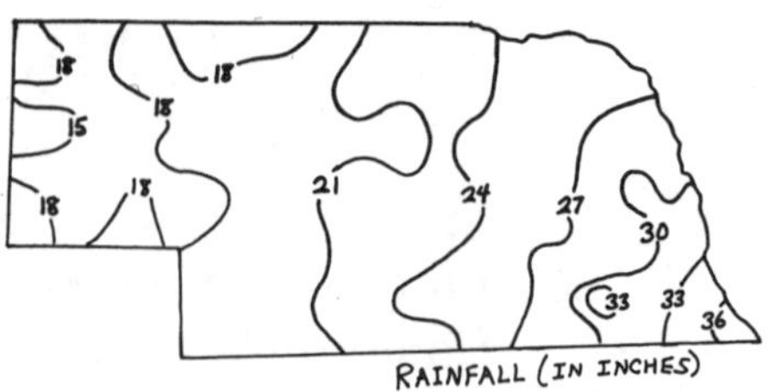

Let me explain the map. If you live near Falls City, in the southeastern corner of Nebraska, you can expect to receive about 36 inches of rainfall during the year.

Near Nebraska City between 33 and 36 inches of rain will fall in a year.

Look farther west. If you live at Ainsworth, you will get between 21 and 24 inches of rainfall in a year's time.

Those of you who live near McCook will receive between 18 and 21 inches of rain.

Look now at Scottsbluff. According to the map, the people who live in that part of Nebraska receive between 12 and 15 inches of rainfall each year.

Isn't that interesting? The rainfall in Scottsbluff is only about one-third of the rainfall in Falls City. No wonder the country around Scottsbluff does not look like eastern Nebraska.

Why is there less rain in western Nebraska than there is in eastern Nebraska? That is a good question. Let's find the answer.

You know that around the Earth there is a mass of air. We call it the atmosphere.

This mass of air, or atmosphere, does not stay in one place. It is constantly moving.

For example, the mass of air moves from west to east across the United States and Nebraska.

When the mass of air comes

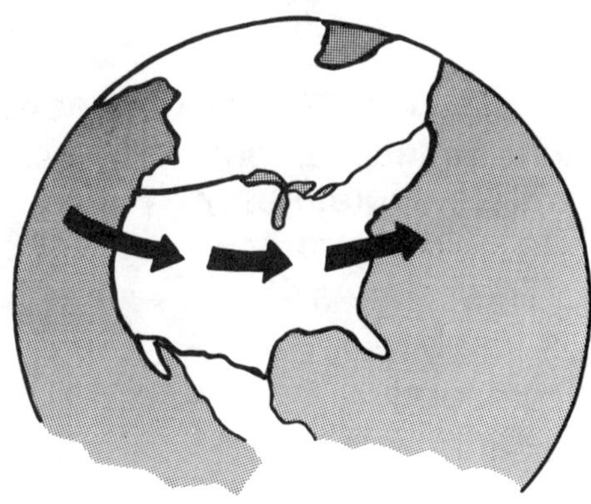

in from the Pacific Ocean, it is carrying huge amounts of moisture. This moisture, of course, was picked up from the ocean.

Then the mass of air strikes the mountains in the western

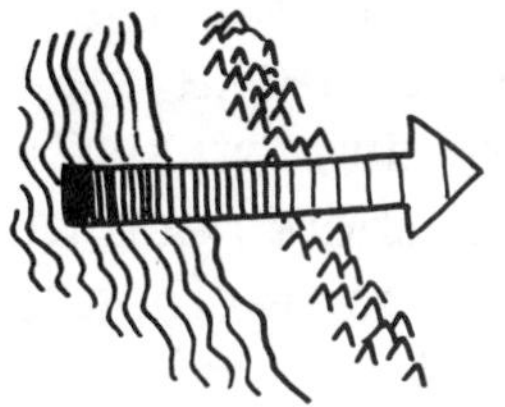

part of our country. The air mass begins to rise. The air cools off, and this causes the moisture to drop from the sky as rain or snow.

As the air mass crosses the mountains it loses almost all of the moisture. So, when the air comes over western Nebraska it is very dry. Very little rain falls.

As the air mass moves east, however, it gathers moisture. Currents of air from the Gulf of Mexico carry moisture northward. By the time the air mass reaches central and eastern Nebraska, clouds carrying moisture have built up. So this means that there is more rainfall in eastern Nebraska than in the western part of Nebraska.

Why is rainfall so important in Nebraska?

I'm sure you all know the answer to that question. It is because Nebraska is a farming and ranching state. Our farmers and ranchers need rainfall in order to raise crops and livestock.

In eastern Nebraska, where there is thirty inches of rainfall or more a year, families can live on small farms. They can raise enough crops to make a living.

In western Nebraska, however, farms must be very large. With less rainfall, they can raise fewer crops. So farms have to be big in order to produce the crops needed to support the farmer and his family.

There is one other problem with Nebraska's rainfall. The rainfall map we looked at shows the amount of rain that *usually* falls.

But as every Nebraskan knows, there can be more or less rainfall each year. More often than not there are periods of drought—years in which less than the usual, or normal, amount of rain falls.

You see how important rainfall is to Nebraska. And you can understand why Nebraska farmers and ranchers are so interested in irrigation.

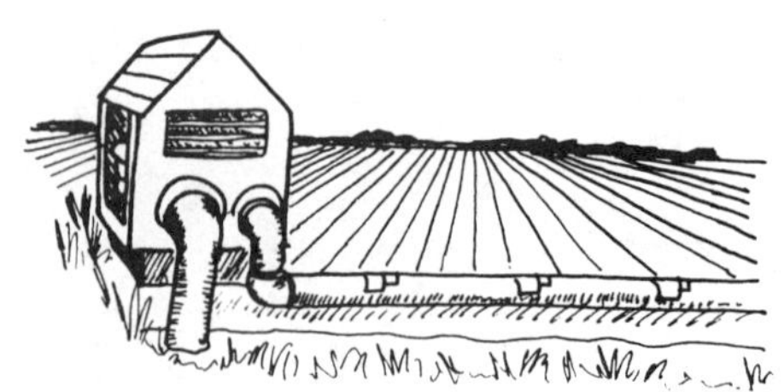

Rainfall is only one part of the weather picture in Nebraska. You know that, don't you?

When we talk about the Nebraska weather we must mention the storms that sweep the prairies. In winter there are blizzards. Often in summer there are hail storms and terrible windstorms. Everyone in Nebraska fears the fierce tornadoes that roar over the land.

And every Nebraskan knows that winters can be terribly cold, with temperatures far below zero. Then comes summer, with temperatures soaring to above 100 degrees.

When the pioneers came to Nebraska they had to learn to live with this weather.

What do you suppose the pioneers thought of the terrible blizzards? What do you suppose they thought of the hot, dry summers?

Yes, they had to fight the rain, wind and sun. We know that many pioneers gave up and left Nebraska. The weather drove them out.

Those who stayed on the land and in the towns prepared the way for us.

"Soil and water are Nebraska's most valuable resources."

"By using the soil and the water wisely, our farmers and ranchers have made agriculture Nebraska's most important industry."

HERITAGE SPECIAL

A Picture To Study.

Study the photograph carefully. Can you answer these questions:

1. Who are the people?
2. Where was the photograph taken?
3. When was the photograph taken?
4. Why was it taken?

Now check your answers with my answers:

1. Who? This is a pioneer farmer and his family. His name is Jacob Graff.
2. Where? The photograph was taken in central Nebraska, in Custer County.
3. When? The photograph was taken some time in the 1880's.
4. Why? See the man to the left with the shovel? He is a well digger. Mr. Graff hired the man to dig a well for the family to use. See the boy in the wagon? See the barrels in the wagon? The wagon and barrels tell us that for many months the family has had to carry their water from a nearby creek or spring. But now they are going to have their own well.

The picture was taken because this was undoubtedly one of the most important days in the lives of this pioneer family.

Water! How valuable it was to Nebraska's pioneers!

UNIT FOUR: THE FIRST NEBRASKANS

"In Unit four you are going to discover some very interesting things about our Nebraska land."

"You are going to discover that our land has a history. And you are going to learn about the plants and animals that lived in Nebraska hundred of years ago."

"And you will discover the story of the pre-historic people who lived in Nebraska centuries ago."

"So, let's go back in time...."

Chapter 9:
Rocks and Bones

As you listen to the land you will hear many interesting stories about Nebraska. For example, in gravel pits and stone quarries you will find stories that took place thousands of years ago.

Workers in stone quarries and gravel pits often find strange looking stones—like this one:

What do you see in this piece of rock?

Yes, there is a clear picture of a fish:

You know what this kind of stone picture is called, don't you? It is a **fossil.**

Here is another fossil.

Now let's look at a third fossil.

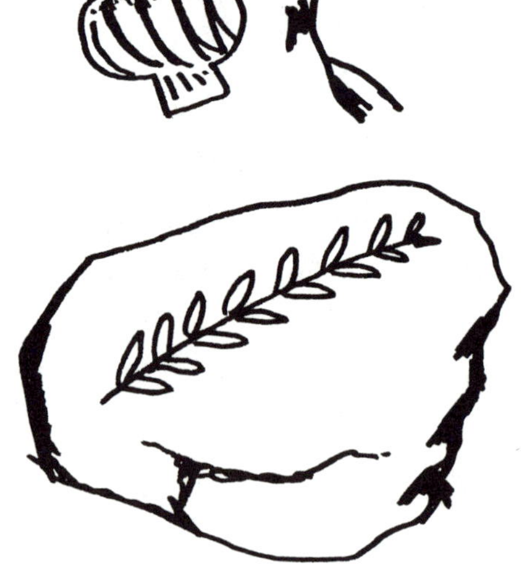

Scientists, who are called **paleontologists,** can tell us about these fossils. They tell us that these fossils show that once Nebraska was a very different land from what we know today.

The fossil fish and fossil shell tell us that centuries ago a huge ocean covered much of what is now Nebraska.

As these animals who lived in the ocean died, they sank to the bottom of the sea. The dead creatures were covered with mud.

Thousands of years passed, and the mud turned to stone. The outlines of the ancient fish and shells remained in the rock.

The fossil of the plant tells us another story—that Nebraska was a warm, swampy place centuries ago. As these plants died they too were buried by mud. The mud became stone and the "picture" of the leaf remained in the stone.

In Sioux County in the northwestern corner of Nebraska, the land has another exciting story to tell us.

Here at the Agate Fossil Beds scientists have discovered the bones of ancient animals. Very carefully the scientists dug up some of the bones. Then they tried to fit the bones together.

Why did they try to put the bones together?

They wanted to learn what these ancient animals looked like. Putting the bones together is like working on a huge jig-saw puzzle.

At the Nebraska State Museum in Lincoln you can see the skeletons which skilled scientists have put together. Once they have finished the skeleton, they cover the bones with material which looks like skin.

Then we can see what the animals looked like when they were alive.

Just think! If you had lived in Nebraska thousands of years ago, you might have run into one of these huge animals. What do you think you would have done had you met one of these fellows?

The bones of ancient animals have been found in many different parts of Nebraska. And fossils are very common. They can be found in many places.

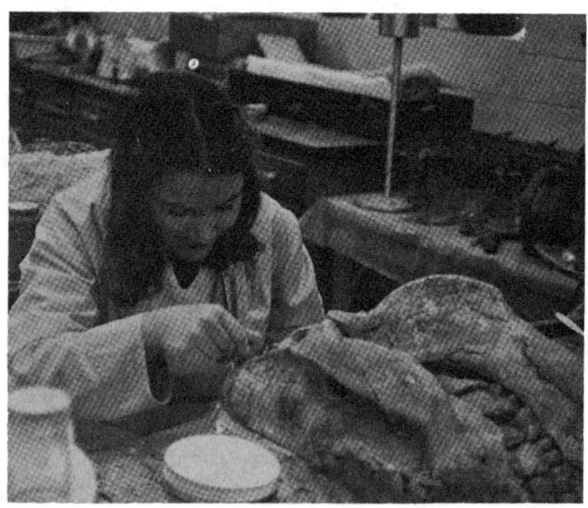

Go to your People Bank and see if you have the names of men and women in your community who collect fossils. These people will be glad to come to your class and show you their collections of fossils.

I want you to meet another scientist—the **geologist.**

Geologists are scientists who study the history of the rocks that make up our Earth. Geologists want to know about the layers of rock and gravel that lie under the ground.

Geologists can tell us some interesting stories about our land. First, they tell us that centuries ago huge sheets of ice moved down from the north to cover parts of Nebraska. These huge sheets of ice are known as **glaciers.**

The huge glaciers moved slowly across the land. They carved out valleys and piled up rocks and dirt to make hills and ridges.

These glaciers had much to do with how the land of eastern Nebraska looks today.

The geologist knows that our Earth is made up of layers of rock and gravel. Deep under the ground there are layers of gravel which hold huge quantities of water. The wells that provide us with drinking water must reach into these layers. The irrigation wells of our farmers and ranches must also reach into these layers of gravel.

In some parts of Nebraska geologists have found oil and natural gas locked up in these rock layers. These pockets of oil and gas may be thousands of feet under the ground. It takes much work and much money to drill the wells that bring this oil and gas to the surface.

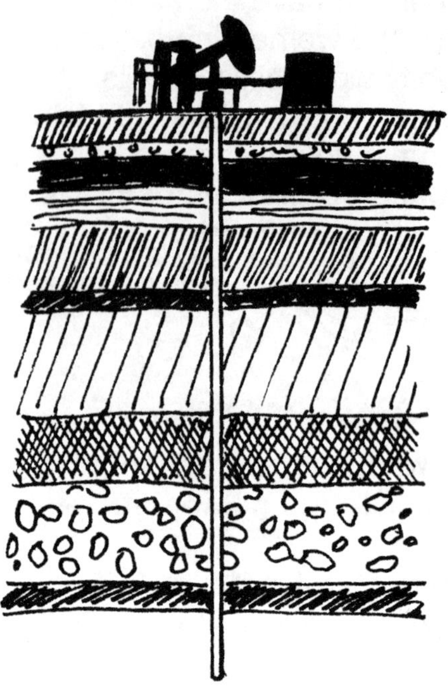

You can see that geologists help us understand the history of our land. They know a great deal about the layers of rock that make up the Earth.

But the most valuable part of our Nebraska land is the soil which lies right on top. It is this soil in which grow Nebraska's valuable crops.

As you travel Nebraska you will notice that there are many different kinds of soil in our State. Some Nebraska soils are brown. Others are black. Some seem to be mainly sand.

Our soils may look different, but all of them are very rich. Wonderful crops can be grown in the soils, but only if there is enough moisture to help the grass, corn, wheat and milo grow.

Soil and water are Nebraska's most valuable natural resources. Farmers and ranchers depend upon the rich soil and upon water. Their wise use of these natural resources has made agriculture Nebraska's number one industry.

Find some person in your People Bank who can tell you about our land and our water. And what about taking a field trip? I know there are many adults in your People Bank who will be glad to show you the land. Perhaps they would also take you on a trip to look for fossils.

This is the goldenrod — the State Flower of Nebraska.

A SPECIAL PLACE TO VISIT...
THE AGATE FOSSIL BEDS

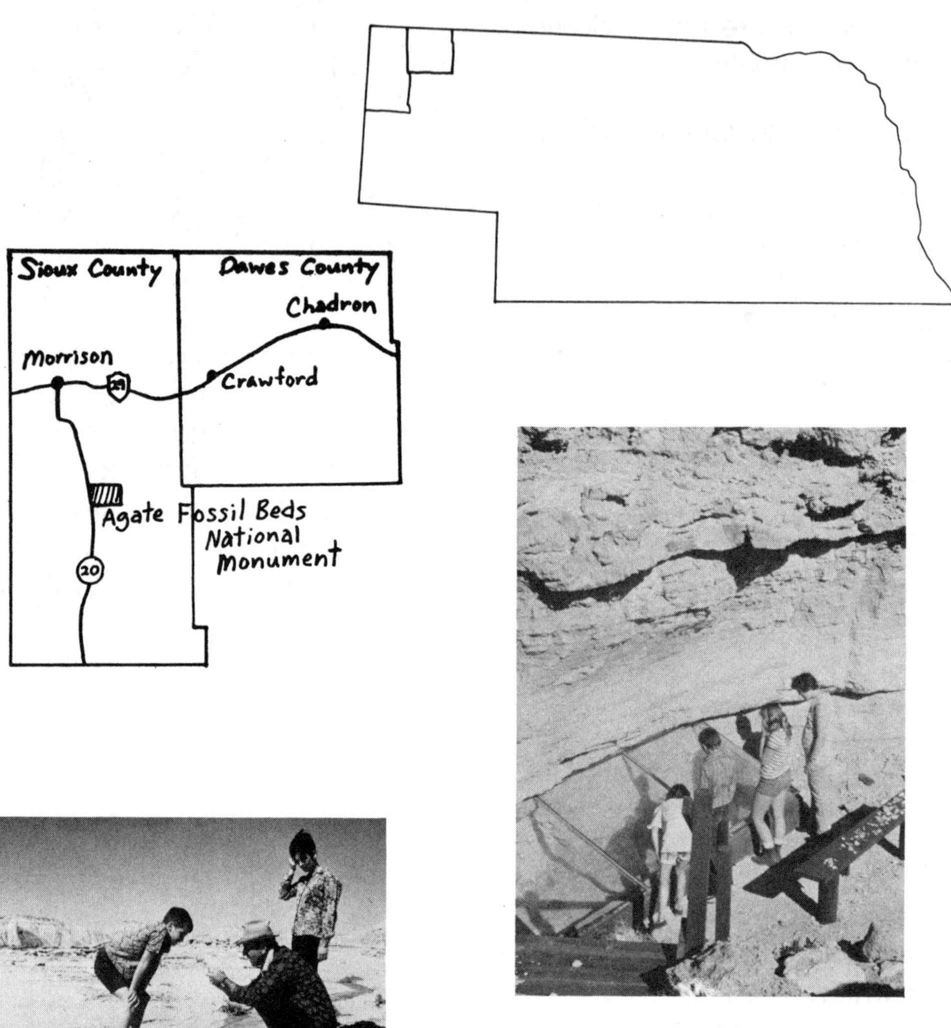

Chapter 10:
Pre-Historic People of Nebraska

"The invention of writing was one of the most important events in the history of our world."

"Once people knew how to write, they could keep a record of the things that happened to them. They were able to write down their history."

People lived on our Earth for thousands of years before writing was invented. These people lived in what we call the pre-historic period. They were pre-historic people.

Some of you probably want to ask a question: "If these people could not write and did not leave written records, how do we know anything about them?"

That is a good question, and **archaeologists** are the people who can answer the question.

Archaeologists study pre-historic people. The way they find out about these people is really interesting.

Archaeologists know that pre-historic people lived by hunting animals. They did not stay long in one place. They had to move in order to find animals to hunt.

When they left a camp, the pre-historic hunters always left behind broken tools, broken weapons and pieces of broken pottery. You might say that pre-historic people were litter bugs.

Centuries passed and dust and dirt covered the old camp sites. Before long there was nothing to show that pre-historic people had once lived at the spot.

Then, hundreds of years later, a man walked by this ancient camp ground. He looked down at the ground and saw something sticking up through the dirt. He stopped and dug up the object.

What had he found? Yes, he had found an ancient arrow head. Archaeologists now come to examine the place. Carefully the archaeologists begin to dig into the ground.

As they dig away the dirt that covers the ancient camp site, the archaeologists hope to find pottery, tools and weapons left behind by the prehistoric hunters.

Archaeologists must be very careful as they dig. They don't want to overlook even the smallest piece of pottery. Everything they find will help them understand how these pre-historic people lived.

Are there any pre-historic sites in your part of Nebraska?

Go to your People Bank and find persons who can tell you about these places. Perhaps you can take a field trip to examine a pre-historic camp site. That would really be exciting!

Pre-historic people lived in small groups or bands. Usually the members of the band were of the same family.

The band camped along streams and rivers where they could get water for drinking and cooking. Women and children picked berries from bushes. They gathered the nuts that fell from the trees; and they looked for plants they could eat.

They lived in huts made from branches and animal skins. In some parts of Nebraska they found caves in which to live. A cave made a very good camp site.

Pre-historic people wore clothing made from animal skins. The clothing was neither warm nor comfortable in the winter. During the summer months they probably wore very little clothing.

The camp was very busy. Women were hard at work preparing food to eat. Some were making clothing from animal skins. It was also the job of women to make pottery out of soft clay. After making the clay pots with their hands, the pots were put in the ashes of the fire to harden.

The men also had work to do. They made tools and weapons out of pieces of wood, stone and bone. This was hard work. It must have taken many, many hours to chip an arrow or spear point out of a piece of stone.

With their crude weapons in their hands, the men left camp to hunt. Only skillful — and lucky — hunters brought back meat. Most of the time the hunters returned without meat.

Once in a while the hunters were able to drive a herd of wild animals, such as buffalo, over a steep cliff. Dozens of animals would be killed, and for a few days the people of the band would have all the meat they could eat.

Life was very, very hard for pre-historic people. They had no medicines to help the sick. They had no way to help members of the band recover from injuries or sickness.

Their greatest enemy, however, was hunger. In dry years they could not find food. The animals wandered off to find grass and water. And the pre-historic hunters had to leave their camp and follow the animals.

As the centuries passed, pre-historic people learned to make better tools and weapons. Even more important, they learned to plant seeds and to raise crops of food.

After they learned how to raise crops, the pre-historic people did not have to spend all their time hunting.

They had time to build better houses in which to live. Their houses were usually made of dirt. Wooden posts held up the roofs.

Gradually the way these people lived changed. They began to have religious ceremonies. Each year at certain times they would hold dances and feasts to honor the god of the rain and the god of the harvests.

The people in the village selected men to be their leaders. The older men of the village taught the boys how to hunt. From the women in the village, the girls learned how to care for the crops and how to prepare food and clothing.

"Life for the pre-historic people of Nebraska was very hard."

"But these pre-historic people were Nebraska's first farmers."

SPECIAL!

Interesting Places to Visit in Nebraska

Indian Cave State Park...

Ash Hollow State Park...

UNIT FIVE: INDIANS OF NEBRASKA

"I want you to meet some very important Nebraskans ...our Native Americans!"

Chapter 11:
Indians of Nebraska

Let's learn the names of the Indians who lived in Nebraska:

Oto	**Pawnee**	**Cheyenne**
Omaha	**Sioux**	**Arapaho**
Ponca		

Now look at the map below. The map shows where these Indian tribes lived in Nebraska.

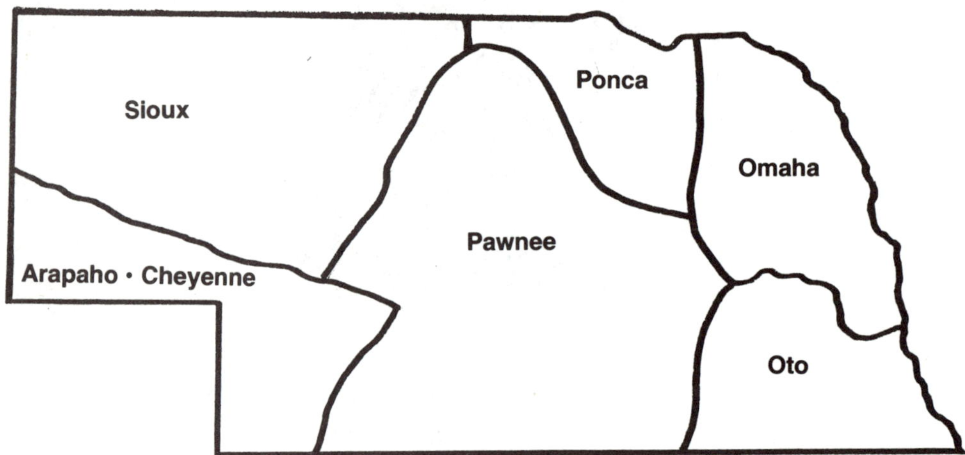

- What Indian tribe lived on the land where you now live?
- Have you heard any interesting stories about the Indians who lived in your part of Nebraska? Tell the class the stories you've heard.
- Are there places or things in your county and your community that are named for Indians? Make a list of the Indian names you find and put the list on your class bulletin board. As you discover other Indian names, add them to your list.

First we need to understand where the Nebraska Indians came from.

The pre-historic people whom we studied in the last unit were probably the ancestors of the Pawnee Indians. If this is true, the Pawnee Indians have been in Nebraska for several hundred years.

The Omaha, Ponca and Oto Indians came to Nebraska from the eastern part of America. As white settlers filled up the eastern part of our country, these Indians moved farther and farther west. Finally they ended up in Nebraska.

The Sioux once lived in what is now eastern Canada. Like the Omaha, Ponca and Oto Indians, the Sioux had to move west. White settlers took their land. They had no choice but to go west in search of new lands upon which to live.

The Cheyenne and Arapaho probably lived in the southwestern part of our country. They came to Nebraska to find a land with good hunting.

"The first thing to remember about the Indians of Nebraska is that most of them came to Nebraska from other parts of our country. Only the Pawnees had ancestors who lived in Nebraska."

When the white pioneers came to Nebraska they discovered that the Indians owned many horses. Horses were very valuable and very important to the Indians. They rode horses to hunt the buffalo. They also used the horses when they fought their enemies.

But the Indians did not always have horses. It was not until about 1700 (just about three hundred years ago) that the Indians obtained their first horses.

You see, there were no horses in America until white men brought them. The first horses arrived with the Spanish explorers and soldiers who landed in Mexico and South America.

The Indians were afraid of the horses. And Spanish soldiers, mounted on horses, won easy victories over the frightened Indians.

The Spanish rulers passed a law that Indians could not own horses. So long as the Indians did not have horses, the Spanish soldiers knew they could easily control them.

Before long, however, the Indians began to get horses. They stole some horses from Spanish ranchers. They also rounded up stray horses that had run away from the ranches.

Then the Indians began to raise horses. Some of their horses they drove north to the lands where other tribes lived. These Indians wanted horses very badly. They were willing to trade everything they owned in order to get horses.

The horses changed the way the Indians lived. Now they traveled farther and faster over the plains in search of buffalo. The horse made them better hunters and warriors. In fact, Indians counted their wealth by the number of horses they owned.

Some questions for you:

1. How did Indians hunt buffalo before they had horses?
2. How did the horse make buffalo hunting easier for the Indians.
3. What weapon is the Indian in the drawing using to kill the buffalo?
4. Was this a dangerous way to hunt buffalo? What could happen to the Indian hunter?

SPECIAL: NEBRASKA'S INDIANS

SIOUX

PAWNEE

OMAHA

CHEYENNE

OTO

PONCA

All Nebraska automobiles have license plates. The first numbers on the license plate tell the county in which the owner of the auto lives. For example, look at this Nebraska license plate:

1-8344	Number 1 county in Nebraska is Douglas County; so we know that the owner of this car lives in Douglas County.

Now, check the license plates below and you'll discover the counties in Nebraska named for Indian tribes.

As you ride across Nebraska in your family car, watch for these license plates. They will remind you of an important part of our Nebraska heritage — the story of Nebraska's Indians.

11-9546	County number 11 is Otoe County — named for the Oto Indians.
39-8346	County number 39 is Cheyenne County — named for the Cheyenne Indians.
54-1934	County number 54 is Pawnee County — named for the Pawnee Indians.
70-9487	County number 70 is Dakota County — Dakota is another name for the Sioux Indians.
80-1156	County number 80 is Sioux County — and named for the Sioux Indians
88-0444	County number 88 is Loup County — named for a family of the Pawnee Indians.

Chapter 12:
The Village Indians

The Omaha, Ponca, Oto and Pawnee Indians who lived in the eastern half of Nebraska were village Indians.

The houses in their village were called earthlodges. An earthlodge was made by covering a framework of branches with sod and dirt.

The outside walls of the lodge were about eight feet high. A domed roof covered the circular house. A hole in the middle of the roof allowed smoke from the cooking fire to escape.

You can easily see why the houses were called earthlodges — they looked as though they were piles of earth.

This is an Omaha earthlodge. How do you think the Indians built this kind of lodge? Do you think an earthlodge made a good house? Why?

Look at the photograph carefully. Do you see the ears of corn drying on the rack? Can you tell what the Omaha women are doing?

They are pounding corn into meal. The woman on the left holds the bowl into which the kernels of corn are put. She then "pounds" the corn into meal with the piece of wood she is holding. The meal will be used to make Indian bread and other dishes.

The Indians built their villages on high ground near a river or stream. A dirt wall surrounded the earthlodges. The wall was a protection against enemy attacks.

Beyond the wall lay the gardens where the Indians planted their crops. After the men prepared the ground for spring planting, the women and children planted the seed and cared for the growing plants.

The Indians did not have garden tools like ours. They used sharp sticks to dig up the ground and to make holes for the seed. They pulled up weeds with their hands.

They raised corn, beans, squash and sunflowers. Corn was their most important crop. Every spring, before the corn was planted, the Indians took part in an important ceremony. There was dancing and singing. The village leaders prayed for good weather and a good corn crop.

Beyond the fields lay the pastures where Indian boys watched the horse herd. They didn't want the horses to get into the gardens and destroy the plants. And they didn't want the valuable horses to wander off and get lost. So the boys watched the animals closely.

A piece of flat ground near the village was set aside as a playing field. The Indians loved games of all kinds. Indian boys had a great time racing their ponies. All of the children, boys and girls, ran races on foot. They wanted to see who were the fastest runners in the village.

The Indians enjoyed having company, and visitors to the village received a warm and friendly welcome. Visitors were seated in a place of honor in one of the big earthlodges.

Then the best food in the village was prepared for the visitors. Usually the main dish was made from corn and meat. For very important guests, the Indian women prepared a dish of stew — made from a fat puppy!

Women of the village had many jobs to do. They worked in the fields. They prepared food and made clothing. The women also made pots, wove baskets and made tools from bone and wood.

The men prepared the gardens for planting. Other than that, the men didn't have other chores in the village. They spent their time talking and planning hunting trips. They also talked about forming war parties and raiding enemy camps to take horses. Much of their time was spent in training their horses and making weapons.

Indian parents loved little children, and they enjoyed playing with their children.

The older children in the camp had many things to do. They learned to sing Indian songs. They learned the dances of the tribe. They were taught to play musical instruments, such as flutes, drums, whistles and rattles.

Dolls made from clay and corn cobs kept the little Indian girls happy. The boys liked to play games such as "snow snake." This game was played in the winter when there was snow on the ground. The game was played by throwing a piece of bone decorated with feathers (this was the "snow snake") back and forth across the packed, hard snow.

Another game was played with poles and hoops. In this game teams of boys tried to toss wooden hoops over a pole.

While the boys and girls played their games, they chewed gum made from the milkweed pod. They sound like modern children, don't they?

Indian children did not go to school as you do. They learned by listening to stories told them by the older men and women of the village.

The children heard stories of famous battles and successful hunting trips. They listened to stories about the great men and women of the village. They heard stories which helped

them understand the land and the wild animals that lived on the land.

Since the Indians did not have a written language, the history of the tribe and the village was preserved in these stories. As they listened to the old men and old women of the village talk, the Indian children came to understand what it meant to be a part of the village. And they learned what they must do to help the village and its people in the future.

The Indian village was a very active place in the spring. Once the crops had been planted, the people in the village prepared for a very important event — the trip to western Nebraska to hunt buffalo.

Careful preparations were made for the long trip to the hunting grounds. The women made skin tipis and prepared food. Men got their weapons and horses in shape and ready for the hunt.

Finally it was time to leave. The skin tipis and bundles of food were tied to long poles which the horses pulled. These were known as *travois* (tra-voy). You might think of the travois as the Indians' pickup truck.

The long line of Indians, horses and travois left the village. Scouts led the way west along the hunting trail.

A few months later the Indians would return to their village. They would bring back packs of dried buffalo meat — enough to last through the winter. After the first frost in the fall, the Indians harvested their corn. The people of the village were now ready for the long winter months ahead.

"The village Indians of Nebraska raised crops and they hunted the buffalo. They did not have an easy life. But they loved and understood this land we call Nebraska."

A SPECIAL NEBRASKAN:

Blackbird, Chief of the Omaha

In this picture you see a band of Omaha Indians along the Missouri River in northeastern Nebraska. Look at the hill in the background. Do you see the mound on top of the hill? That is said to be the grave of Chief Blackbird.

Blackbird was a great warrior, and his people respected and admired him.

One day white traders came to the Omaha village. The Indians eagerly looked over the guns, metal pans, cloth blankets, bottles of paint and piles of beads the traders had brought.

The traders told Chief Blackbird he could take what he wanted from the pile of trade goods — and he did not have to pay for them. That, of course, pleased Blackbird. He liked these traders very much.

A few years later some men in the tribe turned against Blackbird. They said he was no longer fit to be chief. The white traders came to Blackbird and said that they wanted to help him. They gave him a bottle of white powder.

"Just sprinkle this powder on the food of your enemies," they told him. "Soon your enemies will all die."

Blackbird took the bottle of powder — which was poison — and used the powder as the traders had told him. One by one his enemies died.

Once again Blackbird was chief of the tribe. No one opposed him because he had such strong and terrible powers.

Just before he died Blackbird told his people that he wanted to be buried on his favorite horse. He pointed to a high hill overlooking the Missouri River.

"There, on top of that hill, is where I want to be buried," he said.

The Omaha Indians carried out his wishes. After Blackbird died, they placed him on the back of his favorite horse. The horse was killed, and a huge mound of dirt was piled over the chief and his horse.

How much of this story is true we don't know. But today you can visit Blackbird's Hill and see the mound which is supposed to be his grave.

From the top of Blackbird's Hill you look out over the land of the Omaha. Here you can "listen to the land" and hear the story of Blackbird and his people, the Omaha Indians.

Chapter 13:
Indians of the Plains

The Indians who lived on the grass-covered plains of western Nebraska did not live in earthlodge villages. And they did not plant crops.

These plains Indians were *nomads* — that is, they wandered from place to place. Since they depended upon the buffalo for their food, the Indians followed the buffalo herds. The Indians made camp wherever they found buffalo to hunt.

The Indians of the plains lived in skin tents called *tipis.* These tents could be quickly set up and quickly taken down — just the thing for people who were constantly on the move.

Of course, the horse was very important to the plains Indians. On their horses the Indians could travel many miles over the prairie. And it was much easier to hunt buffalo from horseback than on foot.

As you know, the men of these plains tribes were famous hunters and warriors.

How would you like to watch the Indians hunt buffalo? First, imagine you are on a hill in western Nebraska. A herd of several hundred buffalo is grazing quietly on the rich prairie grass.

Look over there! We see the Indian hunters riding slowly toward the buffalo. They move very carefully. They make sure that the wind will not carry their scent to the buffalo. Buffalo can't see very well, but they have a wonderful sense of smell.

The leader of the hunting party signals with his bow. The hunters spread out and surround a small group of buffalo which has moved away from the main herd.

The huge animals toss their heads in the air and turn to run away from the hunters. Their hooves make a noise like thunder as they pound the ground. Huge clouds of dust rise into the air.

Look carefully! We see the Indian hunters among the galloping buffalo. We watch one hunter bring his sweating horse right up next to a buffalo. The hunter draws his bow and sends an arrow into the buffalo — then another arrow — and another.

The leader gives another signal, and the Indian hunters gallop their horses in among the buffalo.

The buffalo stops running. It stumbles and falls to the ground. The Indian leaps down from his horse and gives a loud victory cry. He has killed his buffalo.

The buffalo disappear in a cloud of dust. We see several dead buffalo lying on the grass. They are surrounded by the proud hunters.

Indian women now come running. They begin to skin the buffalo and to cut up the meat. In a short while the meat and buffalo robes are loaded on horses. The Indians return to their camp.

The Indians used just about every part of the buffalo. The meat was their food. The hide was used for clothing and for their tipis. Bones were made into tools. They wasted nothing. I guess you might say that the buffalo was the Indians' supermarket. Everything they needed came from the dead buffalo.

While they were very young, the Indian boys learned how to ride horses. In a few years they were excellent riders. Imagine the skill it took to hunt buffalo from horseback. Remember: the Indians usually rode bareback — without saddles.

Another thing: it took two hands to use the bow and arrow. So, as he galloped alongside the buffalo, the Indian hunter was not guiding the horse at all.

But the Indian horses were well trained. They knew exactly what to do during the hunt. White men who saw the Indians hunt buffalo were amazed by the skill of both the hunters and the ponies.

During the summer months, while they were hunting the buffalo, the Indians traveled in small family bands. Several times a year, however, the family bands came together to make a large camp.

Then the Indians had feasts and celebrations. They sang and they danced around the campfires. They thanked the Great Spirit for sending the buffalo and for giving them a successful hunt.

The leaders of the tribe were chosen because of their ability, bravery and experience. An Indian tribe had many different leaders. Some leaders took charge of the hunting parties. Others led the men on war parties.

These buffalo hunters were great warriors. From time to time war parties left the camp. Usually the goal of the warriors was to take horses from their enemies.

Women had important roles in the tribe, too. In some tribes all of the property belonged to the women.

Some of you have probably wondered how many Indians lived in Nebraska.

There is no way of knowing for sure. But in the year 1800 there were probably about 30,000 Indian men, women and children living in what is now Nebraska.

Yes, the Indian population was very small. All of the Indians in Nebraska in 1800 amounted to the number of persons who live in Grand Island today.

It is fun to learn about Nebraska's Indians. They are very interesting people. I know you will want to learn more about the Indians who lived in your part of Nebraska.

Go to your People Bank. Perhaps you have the names of men and women who can tell you stories about the Indians. If there are Indian men and women living in your community, invite them to class and have them tell you about their people.

In many Nebraska communities there are people who can teach you Indian dances and Indian crafts. I know you would welcome them to your class.

One important thing to remember about Nebraska's Indians. They understood the land.

The Indians lived through hot, dry summers and winter blizzards. The village Indians learned to raise crops. Both the village Indians and the plains Indians were excellent hunters.

They learned to travel across the vast prairies. They learned to talk by sign language to Indians of other tribes. And Indian hunters and warriors used mirrors and camp fires to send messages across the prairie.

"Your study of the Nebraska Indians can help you learn to love the land, just as the Indians did!"

SPECIAL: INDIANS OF NEBRASKA

UNIT SIX: PIONEERS COME TO NEBRASKA

Chapter 14:
Explorers, Traders and Missionaries

Are you learning to "listen to the land?" I hope you are. You can hear exciting stories in every part of Nebraska.

For example, not long ago I drove to Columbus. (Find Columbus on your map of Nebraska.) As I drove into the city I was "listening to the land."

As I "listened" I remembered the story of Pedro Villasur. In 1720 Villasur, an officer in the Spanish army, was sent with his soldiers to chase some French traders out of the Nebraska country.

Near this spot where Columbus now stands Villasur and his soldiers were attacked by Indians. Many of the Spaniards were killed. The survivors fled back to Mexico to report the defeat.

This battle, remember, took place in 1720. You can see that the history of our Nebraska started a long time ago.

The Spanish and French in Nebraska

You may wonder what the Spanish and French were doing in Nebraska so many years ago.

The Spanish, who came from Mexico, searched the prairie country for gold and other riches. The Spanish wanted to find wealth.

"The first white men to see Nebraska were probably Spanish explorers looking for gold!"

The French, who came to Nebraska from Canada, were not interested in gold. They wanted to buy furs from the Indians.

In 1714 a Frenchman by the name of Bourgmont came up the Missouri River. He heard Indians talk about a large river to the north. Bourgmont called this the **Nibraskier** River. This was, of course, the Platte River. In time the word **Nibraskier** was changed to Nebraska.

In 1739 two brave brothers, Paul and Peter Mallet, with six other Frenchmen, paddled their wooden canoes up the Missouri River. They wanted to get to Santa Fe so they could trade with the Spanish.

They followed the Missouri River all the way to what is now South Dakota. They decided that the Missouri River was taking them in the wrong direction. So they left the Missouri River and started to walk south. They crossed central Nebraska. Finally they reached Santa Fe.

The Mallet brothers were the first white men we know about who traveled across our land.

"Just think! Spanish and French explorers and traders visited Nebraska long before there was a place called the United States!"

The Louisiana Purchase

Who owned Nebraska at this time? Spain owned the land for many years. Then the French took it over.

By the year 1800 there were many Americans who thought the United States should own the land. President Thomas Jefferson agreed, and he sent men to talk with the French ruler, Napoleon. Napoleon agreed to sell all of the French lands which lay west of the Mississippi River to the United States.

Look at the map below. The shaded part of the map shows the land we bought from France. The area was called the Louisiana Purchase. As you can see, Nebraska was part of the land which the United States bought from France.

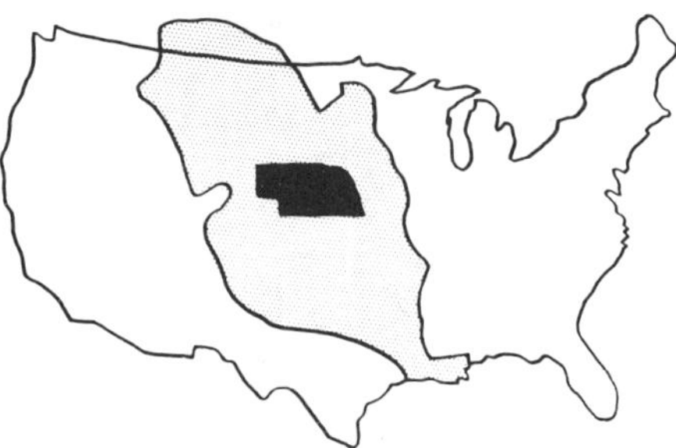

"President Jefferson made a terrific deal. The United States got millions of acres of land — at a cost of only 4 cents an acre."

"By the way, what does an acre of land in your part of Nebraska sell for today?

The Lewis and Clark Expedition

Since no one knew much about the land we had bought, President Jefferson decided to send some explorers to look at the land.

The men he selected were William Clark and Meriwether Lewis. The President told them to take an expedition up the Missouri River, cross the Rocky Mountains and go to the Pacific Ocean.

The Lewis and Clark expedition is one of the most important — and exciting — events in American history. Lewis and Clark, with their forty-three men, had an amazing trip. (There was one woman with the expedition — an Indian woman, Sacagawea, who guided the men through the Rocky Mountains.)

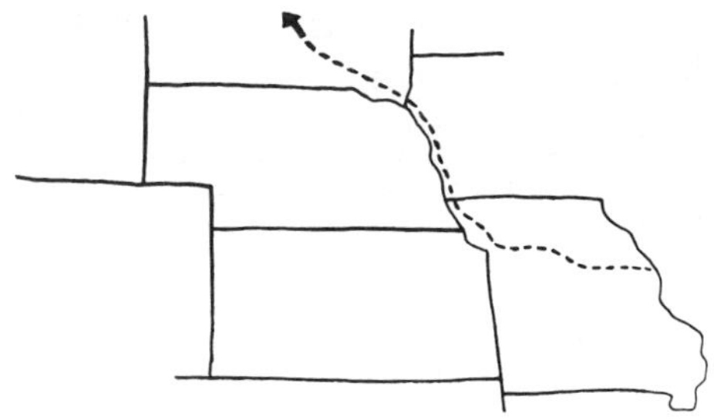

The expedition left St. Louis on May 14, 1804. Ahead of them lay a 4,000 mile trip — to the Pacific Ocean and back. They returned to St. Louis on September 23, 1806.

The expedition followed the Missouri River. The men used a keelboat and two small wooden canoes, known as pirogues. The keelboat carried all the supplies and equipment needed for the long trip.

The thirty men on the keelboat rowed and poled the heavy boat upstream against the strong current. When they couldn't move the boat because of the current, the men splashed ashore, grabbed a long rope attached to the boat and pulled the craft upstream.

It took Lewis and Clark two months to follow the Missouri River from St. Louis to the Platte River in Nebraska. Today we can make that trip by automobile easily in two days.

Lewis, Clark and their men spent six weeks traveling up the Missouri River in Nebraska. They explored the land and studied the plants and animals they found.

On August 3, 1804, Lewis and Clark held a conference with a group of Nebraska Indians. The meeting was held on a high bluff overlooking the Missouri River. This place came to be known as Council Bluffs because of the council held here between the Indians and the American explorers.

1. What is happening in this old drawing?
2. How are the Indians dressed? How are the white men dressed?
3. We know that the Indians and the white men spoke different languages. How did they understand one another?
4. What did the white men tell the Indians?
5. What do you think the Indians told Lewis and Clark?

Pike's Pawnee Village

Another famous American explorer, Lieutenant Zebulon Pike, came to Nebraska at this time also.

Pike, with twenty-two men, marched across Kansas, then went north into Nebraska. In September, 1806, Pike and his men came to a large Pawnee Indian village on the Republican River.

Look on the map and find this Pawnee village.

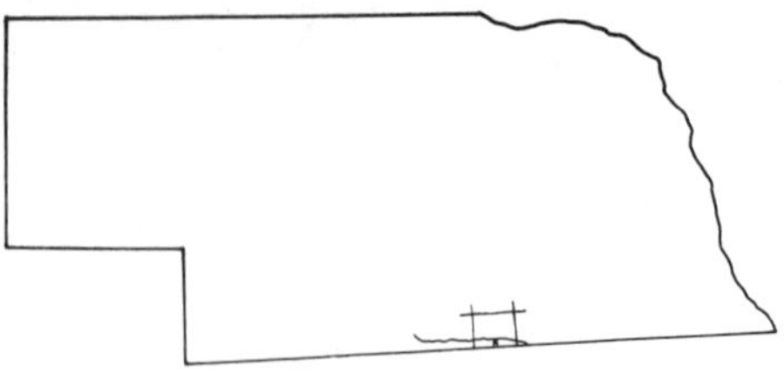

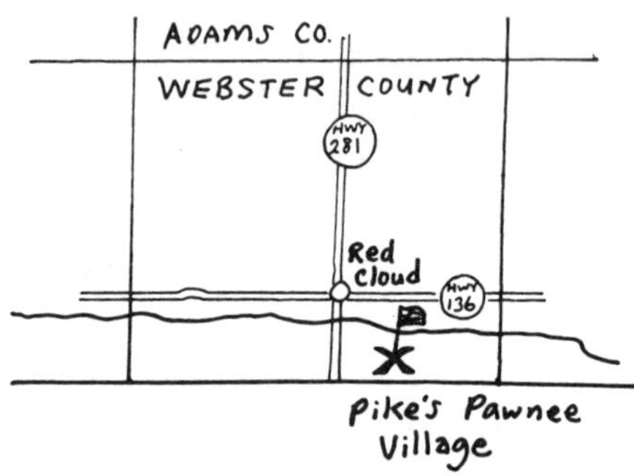

A large Spanish flag fluttered over the earthlodges of the Pawnee. Pike learned that the flag had been given to the Indians by some Spanish soldiers.

Pike talked the Indians into taking down the Spanish flag. He gave them an American flag to fly in its place.

At this Pawnee village on the Republican River the American flag was raised for one of the first times in Nebraska.

The Nebraska Fur Trade

Many fur traders now came to Nebraska. They built trading posts along the Missouri River. Indians brought their furs to these posts. They traded the furs for axes, knives, blankets and guns.

There was an important fur post at Bellevue. This is what that post looked like.

Peter Sarpy operated this fur post for a time. He was one of the best-known traders in Nebraska. Like many traders, Sarpy had an Indian wife. The Indians trusted a white man who had married an Indian woman. And Sarpy's wife, like all Indian wives, was a real help to her husband in his work.

Another important fur post was owned by Manuel Lisa. His post, known as Fort Lisa, was near the Missouri River on the north edge of what is now the city of Omaha.

Manuel Lisa: A Very Special Nebraskan

Manuel Lisa was born in New Orleans. His parents were Spanish. As a young man Manuel began to trade with the Indians. He was very good at his work, and he operated fur posts in many places along the Mississippi River.

About the time Lewis and Clark returned from their famous trip, Lisa decided that the future of the fur trade lay in Nebraska and the West. He traveled up the Missouri River and began to build trading posts.

Lisa was a successful trader because he treated the Indians fairly. Many traders cheated the Indians. Not Manuel. The Indians knew he was a fair man who really liked them. The Indians called him "Father."

Lisa knew that the fur trade would not last very long. White settlers would soon move into eastern Nebraska. Then his Indian friends would either have to move west or find another way of living.

Lisa tried to teach the Indians how to farm. He gave them seeds and showed them how to plant them. He also gave them cattle. His blacksmith made tools for the Indians to use in their fields. But the Indians did not like farming. They wanted to keep on trapping for furs.

For a time Lisa's wife lived at the trading post with him. The Indians never grew tired of touching her white skin and light-colored hair. She was probably the first white woman to live in Nebraska.

There is no question about it. Manuel Lisa, the great fur trader, was a very special Nebraskan.

Fort Atkinson

In 1819 an army of about one thousand soldiers came to the Nebraska country. Led by Colonel Henry Atkinson, the soldiers came to build an Army post along the Missouri River.

Colonel Atkinson wanted to use steamboats to bring his men up the river. But the steamboat had just been invented. The steamers broke down and couldn't move upstream against the current.

So the soldiers came up the Missouri in keelboats. After a long, hard trip the soldiers reached Council Bluffs — the place, you remember, where Lewis and Clark met with the Indians.

They made their camp near the bluff. Many soldiers died of disease that first winter. Then, in the spring, a flood swept away much of their equipment.

The soldiers moved to the top of the bluff and began to build a fort. It was named Fort Atkinson.

For the time Fort Atkinson was a very large Army post. Log barracks were built around the parade ground. The soldiers also built storehouses, a flour mill, blacksmith shop, a brick yard and a theater building.

Near the post there were houses in which the families of the soldiers lived. One building at the Fort was used as a school. This was probably the first school in Nebraska.

Since it was very hard to bring supplies up the Missouri River by keelboat, the soldiers planted large gardens. The crops did very well. The soldiers harvested abundant crops. They were able to send boat-loads of vegetables and grain to other Army posts.

"Here at Fort Atkinson an important chapter in Nebraska's history begins!"

A Special Place to Visit

Fort Atkinson State Historical Park.

Major Stephen Long

In the fall of 1819 Indians who lived near the Missouri River heard strange noises coming from the River. They ran to look.

There, on the River, they saw a strange boat. It made a chugging sound, and gave off lots of smoke. The Indians called it "a fire canoe."

Actually they were seeing the first steamboat to come up the Missouri. This boat, the *Western Engineer,* was something to see! At the front or bow of the boat was the carved head of a serpent or snake. A pipe carried steam from the boiler of the steamboat to the nostrils of the serpent. The serpent seemed to be breathing clouds of smoke.

Major Stephen Long was on the steamboat. He had orders to take a small group of soldiers and scientists west along the Platte River the next summer. They were to make maps of the land they crossed. And they were to make a report about what they saw.

In the spring of 1820 Major Long and his men started out. They followed the north side of the Platte River and went all the way to the Rocky Mountains.

In his report Major Long said that most of the land between the Missouri River and the Rocky Mountains was dry and treeless. He said that farmers would probably never be able to live on the land.

On a map prepared by Major Long's map-maker, the western plains, including much of Nebraska, were labeled "The Great American Desert."

Why did Major Long think Nebraska was desert country? He had lived his life in the eastern part of our country. In the east there was abundant rain and huge forests. When he saw the vast, dry, treeless Nebraska prairie, he must have thought he was indeed in a desert land.

Nebraska: Indian Country

Back in Washington D.C. Congress passed a law which set aside all the land west of the Missouri River — which included Nebraska — as Indian country. Only Indians could live here. No white men could enter the land without permission from the government.

But the law could not be enforced. White traders went into Indian country whenever they wanted to. Most of them gave whisky to the Indians — and that was against the law, too.

Worse yet, the white traders carried diseases to the Indians. Hundreds of Indians died from small pox, mumps and measles. These diseases seldom killed white people; but these diseases just about wiped out entire Indian tribes.

The Missionaries

Churches in the East decided to send missionaries to the Indians. The missionaries would help the Indians become Christians, and they would also teach the Indians how to live like white farmers.

Moses and Eliza Merrill were two missionaries who came to Nebraska. They left their home in Michigan and started for Nebraska. After weeks of difficult travel, they reached the fur post at Bellevue. They were two hundred miles away from the nearest town with white people. The year was 1833.

Mr. Merrill went to live in the Indian villages. He tried to learn their language. He knew that he could not teach the Indians until he learned their language.

In 1835 the Merrills moved into a building that was used as their home and as a school for Indian children. The stone fireplace of that building can still be seen along the Platte River in Sarpy County.

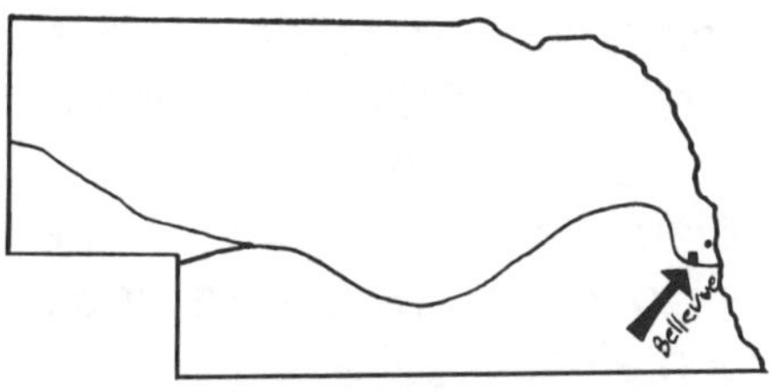

Mr. Merrill slowly learned the Oto language. He wrote several books in the Oto language — a spelling book, a reading book and a hymn book. The hymn book was very important, for Mr. Merrill knew that the Indians loved to sing.

Although they worked hard, the Merrills were not satisfied with their work. The Indians did not want to learn about farming. Most of them were not interested in the Christian religion. The biggest problem, however, was the whisky the Indians got from the traders. Drunken Indians threatened to kill the missionaries and to burn down their house.

Moses Merrill died in 1840. He did not think he had helped his Indian friends very much. However, the Indians did respect him. Their Indian name for Mr. Merrill was "The-man-who-always-speaks-the-truth." Not many white men deserved that name. Mr. Merrill did.

The Platte River Road

Meanwhile, in St. Louis, fur merchants were talking about Nebraska and the fur country. One man by the name of William Ashley decided to hire men to trap beaver in the Rocky Mountains.

The fur traders and trappers usually followed the Missouri River to get to the Rocky Mountains. Ashley had a better idea. He told his men to go up the Missouri River in their boats until they came to the Platte River in Nebraska. Then, they were to leave their boats and use horses to follow the Platte River valley up into the mountains.

Ashley's men laid out a trail which in a few years was used by all the traders. Many of the traders carried their goods in wagons.

It would not be long before covered wagon pioneers, going to Oregon and California, would follow the trail.

An important turning point had come in Nebraska's history. People in the East came to understand that the Platte River valley provided a fine wagon road into the West.

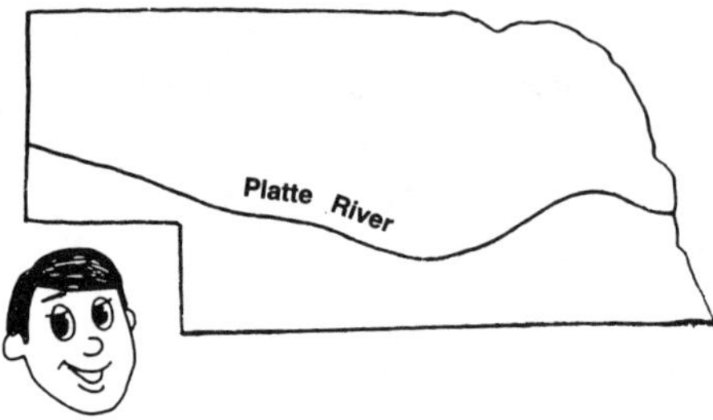

"Nebraska...the great road west. Come to Nebraska and follow the Platte River road to the Rocky Mountains, to Oregon and California!"

Chapter 15:
Covered Wagon Pioneers

The year is 1848. It is early spring in Pike County, Missouri. A cold, damp wind howls around this little log cabin. Inside, sitting close to the crackling fire in the fireplace, the Bidwell family are laughing and talking. Mr. and Mrs. Bidwell and their three children are very excited. In just a few weeks they are leaving for Oregon.

All winter the Bidwell's have been preparing for the long trip to Oregon. Mr. Bidwell bought a wagon from the wagon-maker in town. Since the wagon would be the family's home for the next five or six months, he wanted a wagon that was strong and well-built.

Mr. Bidwell had a hard time deciding upon the animals he would use to pull the wagon. Some men told him that horses or mules were best because they were faster than oxen. The only problem was that horses and mules were much more expensive than oxen.

So, like most pioneers, Mr. Bidwell decided to buy four oxen. Oxen were strong and dependable. And since Indians preferred to steal horses and mules, they were less likely to run off oxen from the wagon train.

Mother Bidwell had been busy too. First, she selected the food they would carry in their wagon. Flour, corn meal, hard bread, crackers, dried meat, dried fruit and vegetables, coffee, tea and cheese — these were the supplies they planned to carry with them.

She also selected the pots and pans needed for cooking. And she bought a small iron stove in which to bake bread. All of these things she put in a large wooden box. Each time they stopped to eat, Father Bidwell would take the box out of the wagon, and she would have everything she needed to make the meal.

Mother Bidwell also filled a medicine box with the medicines the family was likely to need. Then she packed the family's clothing — strong, tough clothing that would take hard wear.

She also packed five pairs of goggles. She heard that trail dust was a terrible problem. The goggles would protect her family's eyes against the burning dust.

Finally, everything is ready. The wagon is loaded, and the oxen are yoked up. Mother Bidwell and the three children climb into the wagon.

Father Bidwell cracks his whip over the backs of the strong oxen. The animals lean forward and begin to walk. The wagon begins to move. Mother sits firmly in the swaying seat. Father walks beside the hard-working oxen. The children, wide-eyed and excited, peek out from under the canvas cover of the wagon.

For the next three weeks the Bidwell wagon slowly follows the road across Missouri. The road is filled with wagons carrying families west.

Finally they arrive in Independence, Missouri, where the Oregon trail begins. Hundreds of wagons are camped around the small town. Thousands of people are waiting to begin the trip to Oregon.

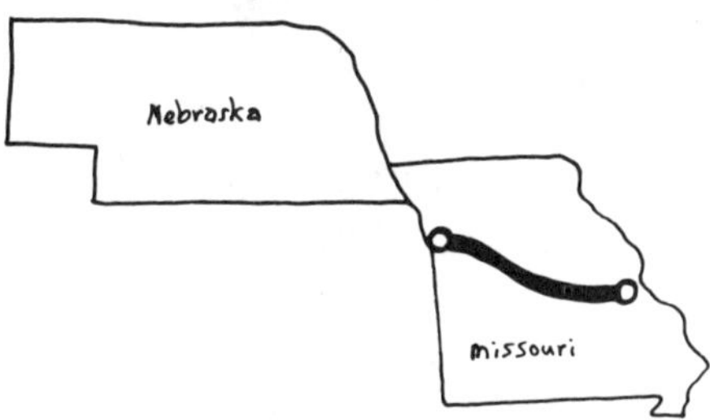

Mr. Bidwell meets with some men who decide to form a wagon train. The men choose Mr. Bidwell to be captain of the wagon train. Then they write the rules for the wagon train. One rule says that every man must take his turn guarding the animals at night. If they lose their animals out along the trail, the pioneers would be in serious trouble.

It is now the first week in April. The new grass has begun to grow on the prairie. The grass is high enough for the animals to eat. Mr. Bidwell rides out to take a look at the grass. He gallops back to camp.

"The grass looks fine to me," he calls out. "Tomorrow we can leave!"

No one in the camp sleeps very well that night. They are all too excited. At first daylight, Mr. Bidwell gives the signal to start. The wagons slowly move into line. The waiting is over. The pioneers are on the trail to Oregon.

An important thing to remember is that almost all of the wagons left Independence at the same time. The pioneers knew they had a long trip ahead of them. So, as soon as the grass was up, they all started out.

The long lines of white-topped wagons covered the prairie as far as one could see. The wagon trains crossed northeastern Kansas. In three or four weeks they crossed into Nebraska. (Please remember that there is no State of Nebraska yet. Nebraska was just wild prairie country in 1848!)

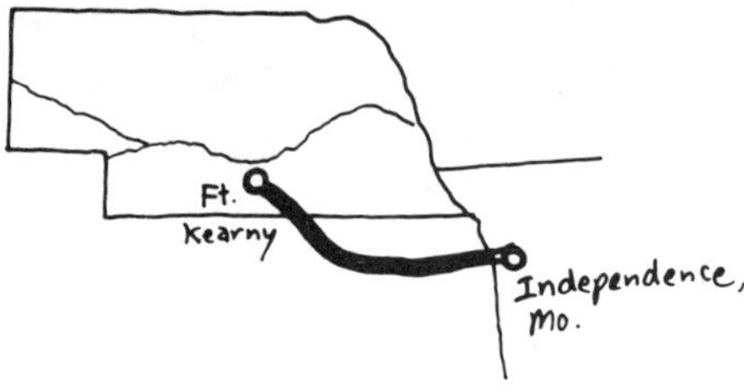

During the first weeks on the trail the pioneers learned many things. Some men discovered that they had loaded their wagons too heavily.

Every day a wagon or two breaks down — too heavily loaded. The animals wear out, too. So the men begin to dump furniture and tools on the ground. The trail begins to look like a gigantic junkyard!

They learned not to waste time. They know that they must make at least fifteen miles each day. There is no time for sightseeing or for side-trips. But most wagon trains do not travel on Sunday. That is a day of rest for the people and their animals.

They also learned about the prairie weather. Heavy rain turns the trails into mud holes. The men spend hours taking their wagons across the wide, deep rivers and creeks. Pulling and pushing wagons through the deep mud at the river crossings is hard work.

The spring storms on the prairie are really something! Few of the pioneers had ever seen a prairie storm with its fierce winds and slashing hail stones.

The oxen often are stampeded by the storm. Then men and boys spend hours searching the prairies for the animals.

Mothers hate the storms. They can't build fires. There is no way to dry wet clothing. Finally, one woman builds a fire under an umbrella and bakes some hot biscuits.

Then there are the bugs! Millions of crickets, buffalo gnats and mosquitoes attack the people and their animals. Some nights no one can sleep because the bugs are so bad. The men build fires and people put their heads into the smoke. The smoke seems to keep the bugs away for a little while.

Something else the pioneers learn — it is not always easy to find a good camping place at the end of the day. Hundreds of people are looking for camp grounds, and there are thousands of animals feeding upon the grass.

Getting a supply of good water is also a problem. Wells are dug along the trail, but these wells are soon filled with disease germs. Unhealthy water causes most of the illness among the pioneers.

Then, there are the accidents. Children fall from the wagons and are run over by the heavy wheels. Men are injured by stampeding animals. At every river crossing there is the danger that someone will drown in the swirling, muddy water.

Guns cause many accidents. Every pioneer family has several guns. They want to be prepared for an Indian attack.

But before long the pioneers realize that the loaded guns are much more dangerous than the Indians. Hardly a day passes without someone being accidently shot. The pioneers decide to unload their weapons and store them in their wagons.

What about Indian danger? The pioneers learned that Indians hardly ever attacked a wagon train. In Kansas and eastern Nebraska Indians visited the trains, but they usually came to trade or to ask for gifts of food.

If a person wandered off into the prairie alone and unarmed, he was asking for trouble. But if the pioneer stayed with the wagon train and minded his business, he would not have trouble with the Indians.

It is not surprising that many of the pioneers became discouraged. Traveling the trail was not easy.

Ask a man why he had decided to give up the trip and he would say, "I've seen the elephant!" This meant he had seen enough problems — disease, bugs, broken wagon wheels, muddy trails, storms and hunger. He and his family were ready and return to their old homes. They had "seen the elephant!"

"Yes, sir. We've seen the elephant. Now it's back to Missouri."

A Day on the Trail

A day on the trail began before the sun came up. While it was still dark, men and boys brought in the oxen from the prairie. The oxen are hitched to the wagons. There is time for a quick breakfast of coffee, bacon and bread.

As the sun peeks above the horizon, the captain waves his hat and the wagons begin to roll. A scout mounted on a fast horse gallops on ahead. He will look for a good camping place. He will also watch for Indians and other signs of trouble.

About eleven o'clock in the morning the wagons move into a circle. The oxen are unyoked from the wagons and led out to graze. This is called "nooning."

The women build campfires and prepare the noon meal. The family sits down to eat beans, bacon and dry bread or crackers.

If the day is very hot this "nooning" period might last until late afternoon. It was best not to use the animals during the terrible heat.

By the middle of the afternoon the wagons are rolling again. If the ground is dry, clouds of dust rise into the air. Now is when the goggles the women packed back in Missouri come in handy. Back home goggles cost fifty cents a pair. Out on the trail a man would give twenty-five dollars to get a pair to protect his eyes.

The wagon train keeps rolling until evening. The scout has found a good camp site, and the wagons leave the trail and circle up.

Evening camp is the best time of the day. First, the pioneers had supper — fresh bread, fried meat, vegetables and a fragrant fruit pie.

After supper, the fun begins. People sit around the campfires and talk. People from other wagon trains drop by to visit. Young people get out their musical instruments, and soon they are dancing on the hard prairie.

One covered wagon pioneer remembered that life in the evening campground was just like life in his village back east. At one end of his camp a young man and a young lady were being married by the preacher. In a nearby wagon he heard the cry of a newborn baby. And out on the prairie men and women were attending the funeral of an old man who died that day.

Yes, life went on in the wagon train just as though the pioneers were still back home in Illinois or Missouri.

The Oregon Trail in Nebraska

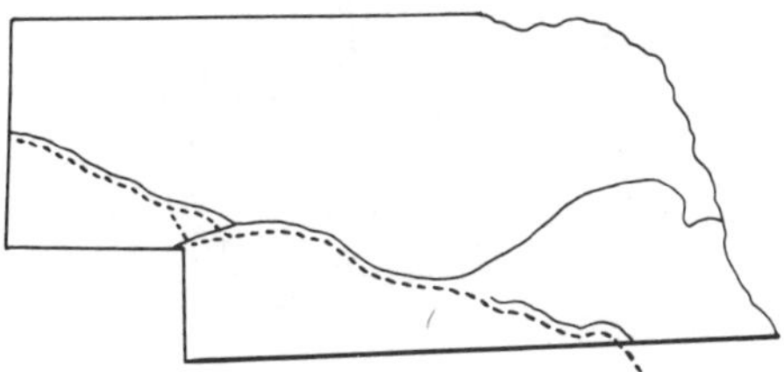

The Oregon trail followed the Little Blue River across southern Nebraska. If the weather was good, the pioneers enjoyed this part of their trip. The trail was easy, and the Nebraska prairie was absolutely beautiful. For the first time the pioneers began to see deer, elk and other prairie animals.

The trail left the valley of the Little Blue River and headed toward the Platte River. The pioneers agreed that the Platte was a strange looking river. "My goodness," said one lady. "Looks as though the water is floating right on top of the ground!"

A man laughed and said, "That's the Platte all right — a mile wide and an inch deep!"

The wagons turned west to follow the river. A few miles ahead the pioneers saw an American flag flying over some buildings. This was Fort Kearny.

Fort Kearny, one of the most important Army posts along the Oregon trail, was built in 1848. Soldiers from the post patrolled the trail and protected the pioneers from Indian attack.

But the Fort was important for another reason. Fort Kearny was a rest stop along the trail. Here there were a blacksmith shop and a wagon shop where the pioneers could make repairs. People who were ill received treatment at the Army hospital. If arguments had come up among members of the wagon train, officers at the Fort would set up a court, hear the dispute and decide who was right.

For the covered wagon pioneers Fort Kearny was the stopping place where they prepared for the next leg of their journey west.

A man at Fort Kearny kept a record of the traffic which passed the Fort between May and September, 1853. Here is what he counted:

3,708 wagons
9,909 men
2,252 women
3,058 children
5,477 horses
2,190 mules
105,792 cattle (This included oxen and beef and milk cows)

The friendly soldiers at Fort Kearny are left behind, and the wagon train continues west. Usually about this time the pioneers saw their first buffalo. This was always an exciting moment! Men grabbed their guns, jumped on their horses and rode off to shoot a buffalo or two.

Hours later the hunters returned, tired and worn out. They had not killed any buffalo. Right then most of the men decided not to waste any more time hunting buffalo.

The trail along the Platte River was wide and smooth. In dry weather the dust was terrible. At the end of the day everyone was covered from head to foot with a layer of fine dust.

The pioneers saw many graves along the trail. Some had died of diseases. Others had been killed in accidents.

The pioneers came to realize that if they were careful about accidents and drank only good water, chances are they would stay healthy.

In fact, most of the travelers said that life on the trail agreed with them. Fresh air (except for the dust), hard work and regular meals made everyone feel in top shape.

As the wagons neared the "forks of the Platte" — that is, the place where the North Platte and the South Platte rivers came together — the pioneers realized that the land had really changed. High bluffs lined the valley. The grass was short and curly. Cacti dotted the ground.

They could not help but notice how dry the air had become. In the dry air the wood in the wagon wheels began to shrink. Spokes fell out and wheels collapsed. At night men took the wheels off their wagons, rolled them down to the river and let them soak in the water overnight. By morning the wood had swollen up and the wheels stayed in one piece.

They followed the South Platte River until they came to a "ford" — that is, a place where the wagon train crossed or "forded" the river.

The river looked about half a mile wide at this spot, and everyone was nervous. But the men whipped the oxen hard. The animals lunged into the water, and a few minutes later they pulled the wagons to safety on the north side of the river.

Once across the South Platte River, the wagons started up a steep hill. The wheels of the wagons cut deep ruts in the ground. Today as you travel along U.S. 30, west of Brule, you can see these ruts very clearly.

A few miles farther north and the wagon train came to Ash Hollow. Here the wagons had to go down a high, steep hill. This was dangerous work. Chains were fastened to the wheels. Ropes were tied to the wagon, and men, hanging to the ropes, tried to keep the wagons from tipping over. The men were very careful, and soon the wagons were safely down the hill.

The pioneers camped in the valley known as Ash Hollow. There was a fine spring of water here, and a good supply of wood.

Next day the wagons rumbled out of Ash Hollow into the valley of the North Platte River. The scouts were very alert. They knew the wagon train was in Sioux Indian country. And from time to time the pioneers saw an Indian warrior, astride his horse, on top of a high bluff, watching the wagon train slowly pass up the valley.

The trail along the North Platte was sandy and hard going. Cacti and soapweed covered the ground. The thorns from these plants were hard on the bare feet of the pioneer children.

And there were many rattlesnakes. At times men walked in front of the teams in order to drive the rattlers off the trail. Pioneers who were low on food sometimes ate rattlesnake meat. Jokingly they called the meat "prairie trout."

Yes, the trail was hard but the scenery was amazing. High rock formations, of all sizes and shapes, lay along the trail. The children had fun giving names to the rocks: Courthouse Rock, Jail Rock, and the most famous of all, Chimney Rock.

Children ran to get a close look at Chimney Rock. They tried to climb it, but the rock was too steep. Most of them took their pocket knives and carved their names in the soft rock.

LARS NELSON WUZ HERE APRIL 1857

John Bidwell Pike Co., Mo. 1848

Buster Ellis 1853

1854

Straight ahead they saw Scott's Bluff. The trail turned south behind this beautiful Bluff. The scenery was wonderful. There were rough, tall rocks to climb. There was a fine spring of cold water. And from the top of Scott's Bluff the pioneers could see in the west the blue outline of a mountain.

Their trip across Nebraska was just about over. Ahead lay the Rocky Mountains. Beyond the Rockies lay Oregon!

The trip by covered wagon across Nebraska took six or seven weeks. The pioneers were now about half way to Oregon. The trail would now take them across high mountains and deserts.

The trip across Nebraska was a very special experience for the pioneers. Here, on the prairie trail, the pioneers learned how to travel in their wagons.

And the pioneers knew that they were doing something very important. Many of them wrote letters to friends back home. Others kept diaries. I'm sure they wanted to keep records of their trips for their children and grandchildren to read.

Today we can ready the letters and diaries of the covered wagon pioneers. They help us "listen to the land" and learn about the covered wagon pioneers.

"The covered wagon pioneers were very important pioneers. They prepared the way for thousands of families who went to Oregon, California and Nebraska!"

Picture Power!

This drawing shows some covered wagon pioneers. Look carefully at the picture and then answer these questions:

1. What time of the year is it?
2. What is happening to the pioneers?
3. What is the man trying to do?
4. What do you think the woman is saying?
5. What do you suppose happened to these covered wagon pioneers in the next two or three hours?

Chapter 16:
Trails West

In the last chapter we traveled along Nebraska's trails with some covered wagon pioneers. They were going to Oregon, remember?

Nebraska's trails led to many other places in the West — California, Wyoming, Colorado, Utah and Montana, just to mention a few.

Wagon trains began to use Nebraska's trails in the 1840's. The trails were used for about twenty years. In the late 1860's the Union Pacific Railroad was built across Nebraska, and the railroad just about ended the days of the covered wagons.

How many persons used the Nebraska trails during those twenty years? The best guess is that about 350,000 men, women and children walked and rode along these historic trails.

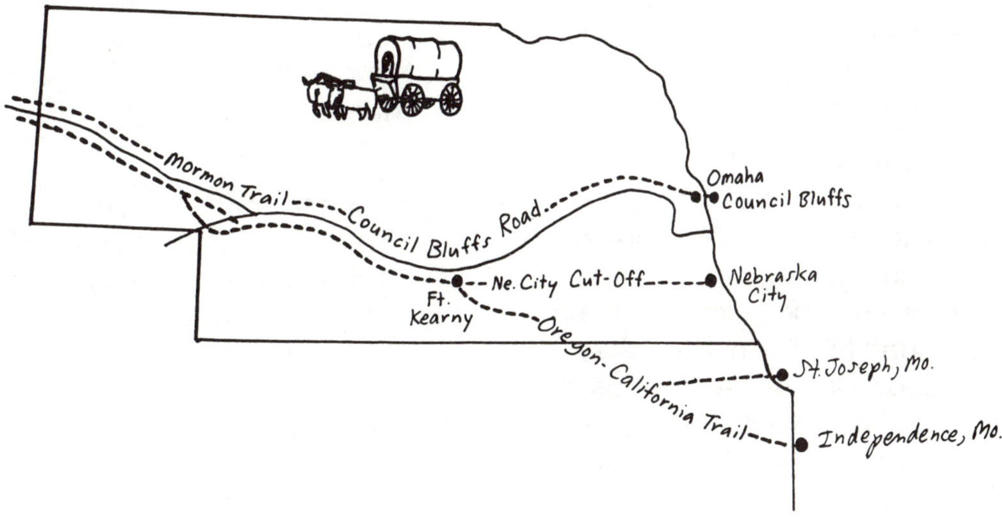

Perhaps you have wondered how the trails were named. First of all, a trail was often named for where the pioneers were going. If they were going to California they called the trail the California trail. Pioneers on their way to Oregon called their road the Oregon trail. So, you see, the same trail could have several names.

Second, a trail could be named for where it started. The trail on the north side of the Platte River was sometimes called the Council Bluffs road. This was because the trail started at Council Bluffs, Iowa.

Third, a trail might be named for the people who used it. For example, the trail on the north side of the Platte River was also known as the Mormon trail, because the people known as Mormons used it.

The Mormon Trail

The Mormon trail was a very famous trail. Let's talk about the Mormon people.

These people belonged to the Mormon church. In 1846 they decided to leave their homes in Illinois. They wanted to find a new place in the West where they could live.

Scouts led their wagon trains across Iowa. Finally they came to the Missouri River. Some of the Mormons made camp on the Iowa side of the Missouri River. Others crossed the Missouri into Nebraska.

The Mormon camp on the Nebraska side was known as Winter Quarters. The Mormons built hundreds of log huts in which to spend the winter. Many became ill, and hundreds of persons died. The dead were buried on a hill west of the camp.

Today you can visit this old Mormon cemetery where historic markers tell you about the hardships faced by the Mormons.

In the spring of 1847 Brigham Young, the leader of the Mormons, led his people west out of Winter Quarters. They followed the north side of the Platte River. They crossed Nebraska and Wyoming and entered Utah, a land where few white men had ever been.

The Mormon trail ended here, in Utah's Great Salt Lake valley. The Mormons began to build a new city — Salt Lake City.

This famous statue of a Mormon mother and father looking into the grave of their baby is found at the Mormon cemetery on the north side of Omaha.

Among the groups of Mormons who later followed this famous trail were the "hand-cart" pioneers. Too poor to buy oxen and covered wagons, these Mormons made two-wheel carts out of wood. They piled their little children and their belongings in these hand-carts. Then they pushed and pulled the carts all the way to Utah.

The Gold Rush Trails

Between 1849 and 1851 more than 150,000 persons crossed Nebraska. Where were they going? They were on their way to dig for gold in California.

Since gold was discovered in 1849, these gold-seekers called themselves "forty-niners." They were young men and old men; rich and poor. But they all had "gold fever." They wanted to get to California and "strike it rich!"

Among the "forty-niners" was a young man by the name of George Winslow. He lived in Newton, Massachusetts. He left his wife and two little boys and took off for California with twenty-four of his friends.

George and his friends traveled by railroad and steamboat to Independence, Missouri. Here, at this "jumping-off" town, they purchased mules and

Here is what the Mormon hand-cart pioneers looked like.

wagons. (Remember: men in a hurry used mules or horses to pull their wagons. Oxen were too slow for "forty-niners.")

On May 14, 1849, George and his friends left Independence and started for California.

Like all the "forty-niners," these young men from Massachusetts did not know much about traveling on the trail. They had many difficulties. The worst thing was that George became very ill. His friends cared for him as best they could. But George died. His friends buried him along the Nebraska trail.

Today you can visit George Winslow's grave. It is located in Jefferson county, just north of Fairbury. As you walk to the grave you will see the ruts left by the covered wagons.

The Pike's Peakers

Another gold rush came in 1858. This time gold was discovered in Colorado. Since the gold mines were near Pike's Peak, the gold-seekers called themselves "Pike's Peakers."

Many of the "Pike's Peakers" started their journey across the plains from towns in Nebraska — places like Nebraska City, Plattsmouth and Omaha.

The men usually came to these towns by steamboats which operated on the Missouri River. After buying supplies, wagons and animals, the gold-seekers headed for Colorado.

On the canvas tops of their wagons men painted the words, "Pike's Peak or Bust!" Months later many returned along the trail. They had not found any gold. On the faded canvas they now had written, "Busted, By Gosh!"

There were interesting sights to be seen on this gold rush trail. One man walked all the way to Colorado. He pushed a wheelbarrow in front of him. In the wheelbarrow were fifty pounds of flour, twenty-five pounds of bacon, a pick, a shovel, a tin pan for washing gold dust out of the dirt and all his camping equipment. It was quite a load to push all the way to Colorado.

There were women who followed the trail, too. The most surprising thing about these women gold-seekers is that they wore men's pants and shirts. They found that long dresses were too uncomfortable for traveling the trail.

The Black Hills Gold Rush

Another gold rush trail was laid out in the 1870's. This Nebraska trail led to the gold fields in the Black Hills of South Dakota.

Since the Union Pacific Railroad operated across Nebraska at this time, the gold-seekers took the train to Sidney. At Sidney they got off the train and took the trail north to the Black Hills.

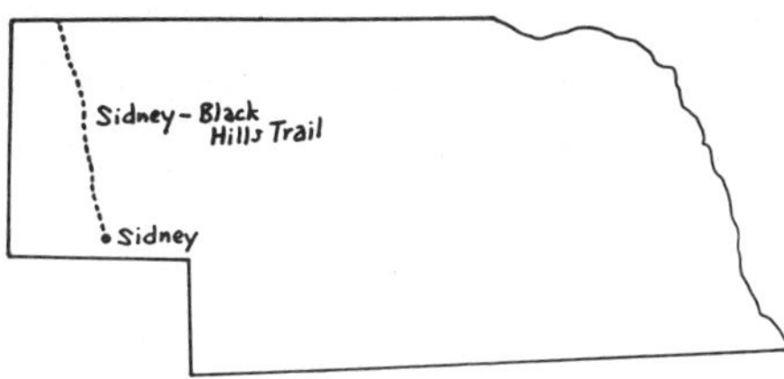

During the days of the gold rush Sidney was a wild, lawless town. There were many saloons and gambling houses where men spent their time and money.

It is said that there was one dance hall in Sidney where a fight started one night. Shots rang out and a man fell dead. The body was dragged to a corner and the dance went on.

Then, a little later, more gunfire and another body lay on the floor. The second body was also dragged into the corner and left. The folks went on with their dancing.

After a short while — you guessed it — another fight, another gun shot, another body. After the third murder, the men and women left the dance hall. The party was over!

Now, chances are this is just

a story. But the truth is, Sidney was a pretty wild place back in the gold-rush days.

Fort Sidney, an Army post, stood near the town. The fort had been built in 1867. Soldiers from Fort Sidney protected the workers who built the Union Pacific Railroad across western Nebraska.

When the Black Hills gold rush started, soldiers were sent to patrol the trail. Robbers held up the stagecoaches and robbed the men and women who traveled the trail. Soldiers and law officers did the best they could to protect the trail. But they did not have an easy job.

Indians and Soldiers

The covered wagon pioneers knew that they would meet Indians along the Nebraska trails. Many probably expected to fight the Indians.

The Indians they met in eastern Nebraska, however, were almost always friendly. The Indians rode up to the wagon trains. They looked into the wagons. They touched the clothing of the white folks. The pioneers realized that the Indians were friendly and very, very curious.

In the early days the Indians often helped the pioneers. The Indians showed them where to find grass and water. They traded horses with the pioneers — and the white men learned that the Indians were sharp traders. They would not be cheated.

But the white people also learned not to wander around on the prairie alone and unarmed. That was a very dumb thing to do. A party of Indians, not as friendly as those who visited the wagon trains, might find the person, rob him — perhaps even murder him.

Another important thing — the pioneers learned to watch their animals carefully. Even the friendly Indians were likely to run off horses, mules and oxen if they had the chance.

During the 1840's and 1850's the covered wagon pioneers had little trouble with the Indians. But as more and more wagon trains crossed the prairies, the Indians in western Nebraska became angry.

The United States government sent men to talk with the Indians. They told the Indians not to bother the white pioneers. If the Indians behaved, they said, the government would give them money and presents.

The Indians signed treaties and agreed to allow the wagon trains to pass safely through their country. In return, the government promised to give them food and other supplies.

But neither side lived up to the agreements. The Indians became more and more angry.

In 1854 a wagon train approached Fort Laramie. (Find Fort Laramie on the map. It is in Wyoming, just a few miles out of Nebraska.)

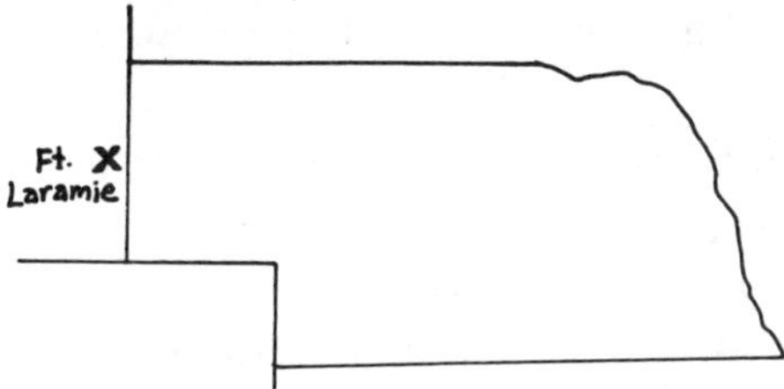

A lame cow limped along behind the wagon train. Suddenly, a band of Indians rode up and drove off the cow. They chased the animal to their camp along the North Platte River.

The owner of the cow hurried into Fort Laramie. He told the soldiers what had happened. Lieutenant John Grattan and twenty-eight soldiers were sent to get the cow back.

Grattan and his men rode into the Indians' camp. There was an argument, and the soldiers began to shoot. In a few minutes the battle was over. All the white soldiers lay dead.

The Indians quickly fled north into the hills. They knew the white men would be very angry.

The next year an army marched up the North Platte valley. General William S. Harney was in command. He and the soldiers came to punish the Indians who had killed Lieutenant Grattan and his men.

Harney's scouts found an Indian camp north of Ash Hollow. The soldiers attacked the camp. Many Indian men, women and children were killed. Many others were taken prisoner by the soldiers.

The Indians were now very frightened. They did not want to have a war with the white soldiers. So, for a few years the Nebraska prairie was peaceful and quiet. The covered wagons rolled over the trails, and the pioneers had no trouble with the Indians.

An Interesting Place to Visit!

Fort McPherson National Cemetery

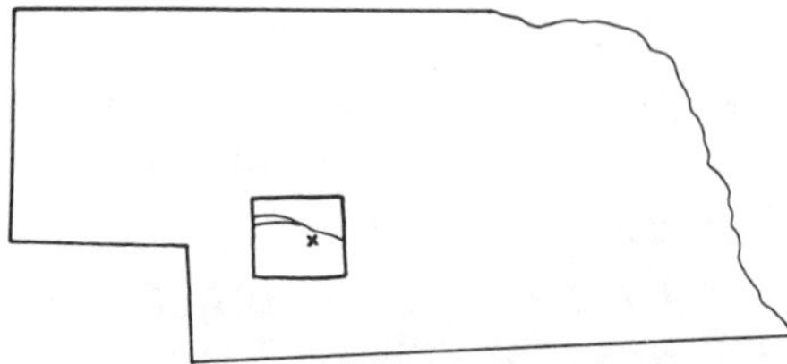

In 1861 the Civil War began. Soldiers who had been stationed along the trail were sent east to fight in the war.

The Indians then took to the war path. Only large wagon trains with well-armed men could travel safely. There were many weeks when the Indians completely closed the trails.

The few soldiers who were at Fort Kearny and Fort Laramie did what they could to protect the wagon trains. And in 1863 the Army built another post in Nebraska. They named the new post Fort McPherson.

The truth is, there were never enough soldiers to protect the trails. And the soldiers were poorly trained. Many did not have good weapons.

It is not surprising that scores of soldiers deserted — that is, they ran away from the Army. Indian warfare was very dangerous and very difficult. The $12.00 a month the soldiers received was not enough to make them want to fight the Indians.

The Civil War ended in 1865. The Army now had soldiers they could use to fight the Indians. For the next twenty years the Indians and the white soldiers fought a long and bloody war. Most of the battles were fought outside Nebraska.

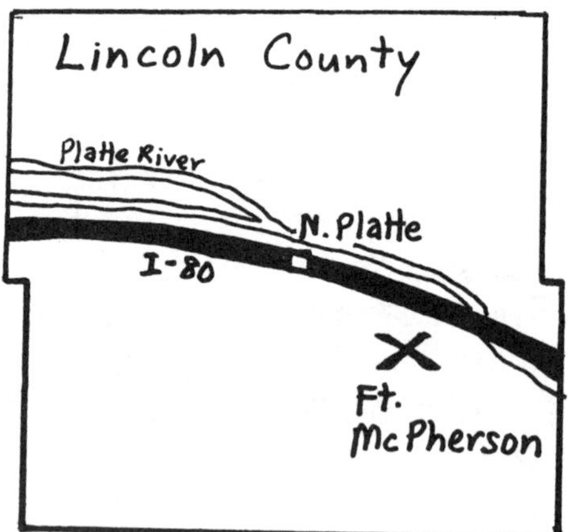

The Bullwhackers

The western country was now beginning to change. Towns were springing up on the prairies and in the mountains. There were mining camps, ranches and Army posts too.

These settlers needed supplies from back east. Machinery, food, clothing — everything they needed had to come from eastern stores and factories.

Big steamboats brought the goods up the Missouri River to towns in Nebraska. The steamboats unloaded their cargoes on the busy docks.

The boxes, bags and barrels were loaded into huge freight wagons. Drawn by eight or ten oxen, these freight wagons then set out on the long trip across the plains. Weeks later the freight wagons rumbled into the towns, mining camps and Army posts where the supplies were needed.

The men who drove the freight wagons were known as "bullwhackers." They walked beside the oxen and "whacked" the animals with sticks and whips.

Carrying freight across the plains became an important business. One of the largest companies, Russell, Majors and Waddell, had its headquarters in Nebraska City.

In 1860 this company owned five hundred freight wagons and five thousand oxen. The wagons carried more than three million pounds of freight that year.

Mr. Majors, who lived in Nebraska City, was a very interesting man. To every man who worked for the company Mr. Majors gave a Bible. He also had a list of rules the bullwhackers were expected to obey: no whisky drinking, no card playing and no swearing. Above all, he told his men, they were to take good care of their animals and they must treat the Indians they met with kindness.

Mr. Majors paid his men twenty-five dollars a month, which was very good pay for that time.

There were many freighting companies in Nebraska. Some were large outfits, others were small. During the summer months long lines of freight wagons filled the trails. Mrs. MacDonald, who lived near Fort McPherson, said that freight wagons continually passed her house, one after another, from sunrise to sunset.

Some of the freighters carried unusual cargoes. One man learned that the Colorado miners were having trouble with mice and rats. So this smart fellow loaded up all the stray cats he could find — about two hundred of them. He crossed the plains with this howling and yowling cargo. In the mining camps he sold each cat for ten dollars. He made a good profit in the deal.

The freighters' trail which ran west out of Nebraska City was called the Nebraska City cut-off. After reaching Fort Kearny, the freighters followed the regular trails along the Platte River.

In 1862 a man by the name of Brown arrived in Nebraska City. He brought with him a huge steam engine on wheels. This is what his "steam wagon" looked like.

Mr. Brown said that his steam wagon would pull four or five loaded freight wagons. He also said that his engine could pull the wagons faster than oxen or mules could.

So, while the interested citizens of Nebraska City watched, he hitched up a line of wagons to his steam wagon and started out on the trail. Four miles west of Nebraska City his steam wagon broke down. That was the end of the steam wagon. However, the trail from Nebraska City now became known as the Steamwagon Road.

Back in the days of overland freighting Nebraska City must have been a very exciting place. Look at this old drawing of Nebraska City. What do you see in the picture?

Just how busy was Nebraska City when this drawing was made? In the year 1865 freighting companies in Nebraska City employed 8,385 men and owned 7,365 wagons, 7,321 mules and 50,712 oxen. In that year the companies carried 31,445,428 pounds of freight. Freighting was, indeed, a very big business!

Road Ranches

Each year more and more people used the trails. Some smart men had an idea. Why not open businesses along the trails — places where travelers might buy supplies, meals and lodging?

Before long such places did appear along all the trails. The pioneers called them road ranches.

Here is an advertisement, printed in 1860, for a road ranch which was located on the Council Bluffs road:

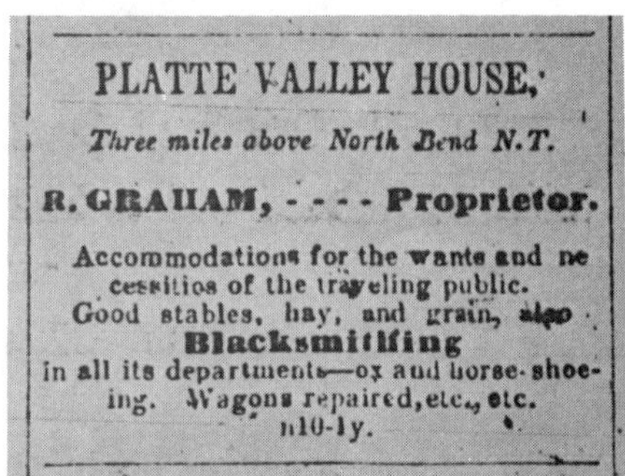

Travelers were glad to see the road ranches along the trail. They were located about fifteen or twenty miles apart, just the distance a person could travel in a day. It was nice to know that you could buy food along the trail and that there was a place you could shoe your horses or repair your wagon.

Of course, some of the road ranchers were not very honest. They sold poor goods and charged very high prices.

But the road ranches were a real help. They made traveling over the trails much easier.

Look at this interesting old photograph. This is the Cheese Creek road ranch on the Nebraska City cut-off or Steam wagon road. A man and his wife operated the ranch. Can you find them in the picture?

They made cheese and sold it to passing travelers. They became well known for their excellent cheese. This is how the ranch got its name, and the name, Cheese Creek, was also given to a nearby stream.

People In A Hurry!

As the years passed people no longer wanted to travel in the slow wagons pulled by oxen. No, people were in a hurry. They wanted to go west — fast!

Another thing! Miners, ranchers and townspeople wanted to get mail. They could hardly wait to hear from their friends and relatives in the East. They demanded that the government deliver their mail to them as fast as possible.

So, stagecoach companies were formed, and the government paid the companies to carry the U.S. mail. The stages also carried passengers. It was a very important and interesting business.

In the 1850's stagecoaches operated out of Omaha and other towns in eastern Nebraska. The stages carried mail and passengers across the plains to Colorado, California, Utah and many other places.

The stage companies built stations every fifteen or twenty miles along the trail. Here fresh horses or mules were hitched to the stagecoach. The passengers had a few minutes to dash into the station for something to eat. Then, it was back into the coach and off down the trail.

Stagecoaches had seats for nine passengers. Another four or five might ride on top of the coach. That was a very dangerous and uncomfortable place to ride.

There is only one word to describe a stagecoach ride — *rough!* The coach bounced and swayed. Passengers were thrown from one side to the other. It is said that if a passenger managed to live through the first day of his trip, he had a pretty good chance of making it to the end of the line.

Passengers were not happy with the food they received at the stations either. At one Nebraska station, dinner consisted of a few pieces of greasy meat, a chunk of week-old bread and a cup of milk — filled with dead flies!

The stage drivers were colorful characters. They were skilled drivers who knew how to handle horses and mules. It took a good driver to keep a stage on schedule. Usually they averaged about nine miles an hour through all kinds of weather and over all kinds of roads.

In California there was a well-known stage driver, Charlie Parkhurst. He was one of the best. It wasn't until Charlie died that his friends made an interesting discovery — Charlie was a woman.

Stagecoach travel was not cheap. The five or six day trip from Omaha to Denver, Colorado, cost $175. The cost of riding from Omaha to California was $600. This was a two weeks' trip. Meals, such as they were, cost extra.

Yes, a jolting, jarring, dusty trip in a statecoach was no picnic. For weeks after their trip statecoach passengers complained of sore muscles and aches and pains.

But for folks in a hurry, the stagecoach was the best way to travel to the western trails.

The Pony Express

The most famous mail service on the plains was provided by the Pony Express. Men riding fast, tough ponies carried the mail from St. Joseph, Missouri, to Sacramento, California. They made that 1,950 mile trip in just ten days.

The Pony Express began operations in 1860. Sixty young riders were hired to carry the mail. The riders were small men. None weighed more than 130 pounds.

Each rider rode a forty-five mile section of the trail. At the end of his forty-five mile stretch, the rider handed the leather *mochila* which held the letters to the next rider.

Pony Express stations were set up about every fifteen miles. The riders changed horses at these stations.

It must have been exciting to see a Pony Express rider gallop up to a station! He pulls his sweating horse to a stop and leaps to the ground. He throws the mochila on the fresh horse that is waiting for him. Then he jumps into the saddle and he is off down the trail. All this would take only two or three minutes.

How much did it cost to send a letter by the Pony Express? For a letter that weighed one-half ounce — and that is not a very big letter — the charge was between $2.50 and $5.00.

The Pony Express went out of business after only eighteen months. That isn't very long, but the Pony Express is an interesting part of our Nebraska heritage.

We should remember the men who rode for the Pony Express. James Moore rode 280 miles in fourteen hours. Bill Cody (later to be known as Buffalo Bill) in an emergency carried the mail 230 miles. Then there was Jack Keetley who, on a bet, rode 340 miles in 31 hours — without stopping once to rest.

The riders went through in all kinds of weather. No matter what they faced — rain, snow, mud or dust — the riders did their jobs. Only once was a packet of mail lost. All other letters arrived safely at their destinations.

The telegraph wire, strung across the plains, put the Pony Express out of business. The metal telegraph wires carried messages much faster than could the gallant men and horses of the Pony Express.

From Trail to Rail

In the 1840's covered wagons rolled across the Nebraska trails. Then came the bull-whackers, the stagecoaches and the Pony Express. Next, the wires of the telegraph were strung across Nebraska. And in 1869 a person could ride from Omaha to California in a rail-road train.

Just think! From covered wagons to the railroad in just thirty years!

The covered wagon trails had been very important to Nebraska. In the first place the covered wagon pioneers who followed the trails learned about our land. Most of them understood that Nebraska was not a desert land at all.

The covered wagon pioneers wrote letters to their friends in the East. They talked about the fertile soil and the beautiful land. People began to hear good things about Nebraska.

The road ranchers were important, too. They were the first persons to settle in Nebraska. They planted crops and herded animals on the prairie. They proved that Nebraska was a land where farmers could live.

For years Nebraska had been a country the covered wagon pioneers crossed as they went to Oregon, California and Colorado. But now Americans began to see Nebraska differently. More and more persons thought about coming to Nebraska. They thought about building towns and making farms.

A new generation of pioneers was on the way: the men, women and children who would build the State of Nebraska. The covered wagon pioneers prepared the way for these new pioneers.

"From covered wagon trails to railroads in just thirty years! And the iron rails, laid on the prairie, were to be the trails which brought the pioneer town-builders, farmers and ranchers to Nebraska."

UNIT SEVEN: THE PRAIRIE PIONEERS

"Tell your friends and relatives in Europe and in the eastern States!"

"Yes, tell them to come to Nebraska…THE LAND OF THE PRAIRIE PIONEERS.

Nebraska in 1854

In 1854 many people were excited about Nebraska. They had heard good things about the land which lay west of the Missouri River. They wanted to buy land in Nebraska, and many wanted to build towns in the new land. They all believed that there was money to be made in Nebraska.

Steamboats chugged up and down the Missouri River regularly. Each boat brought people from the East who wanted to move into Nebraska. These anxious people had to wait in Iowa and Missouri towns for Nebraska to be opened to settlers.

Then, in January, 1854, Congress passed a law which said that settlers could move into Nebraska. The law also set up Nebraska Territory. A government was formed which would run Nebraska Territory. After more people moved into Nebraska, a state government would be established.

Although people were excited about moving to Nebraska, there was one problem. Most of the settlers, back at this time, believed that the prairie land which lay west of the Missouri valley was not good land. They thought that the treeless plains could not be farmed.

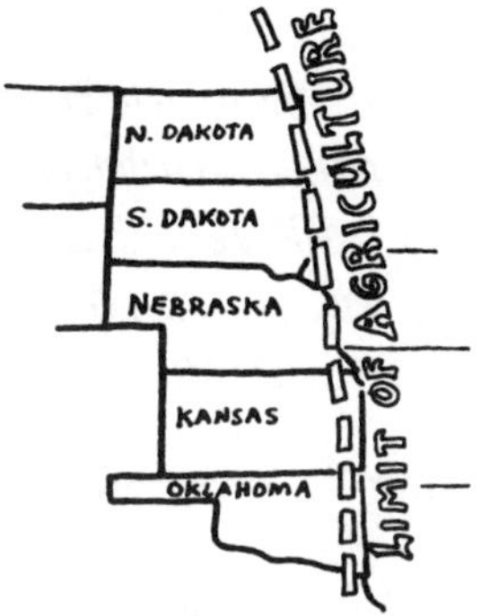

"Limit of agriculture." "Many maps at this time showed a dotted line that marked the point beyond which farming was not possible.

But in 1854 the excited pioneers did not worry about the treeless prairie lands. They wanted to come to Nebraska and get busy building towns.

"I'd like you to meet a good friend of mine. She is another Nebraska pioneer, and her name is Tina Tree-planter."

"Hi, boys and girls. I'm glad to meet you. Billy has told me a lot of good things about you.

"Now it is my turn to help you learn about Nebraska and our prairie pioneers.

"You know that very few trees grew on the Nebraska prairie. Prairie fires burned off all the trees that tried to grow.

"So the pioneers set to work planting thousands of trees. They knew that trees would provide firewood and fence posts. They also believed that trees might cut down the wind and would bring more rainfall.

"But more important, trees just made the country look better.

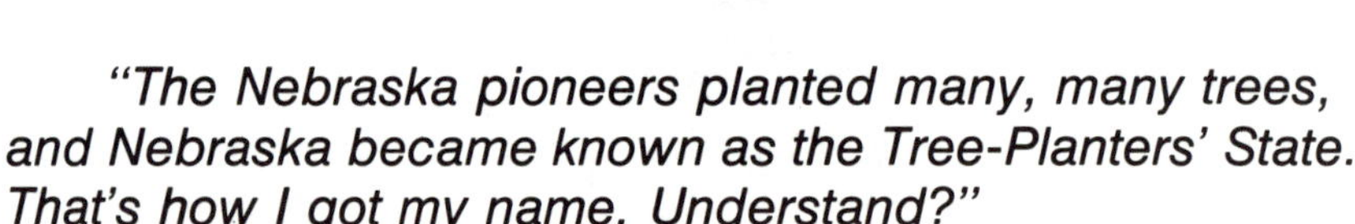

"The Nebraska pioneers planted many, many trees, and Nebraska became known as the Tree-Planters' State. That's how I got my name. Understand?"

Nebraska Facts

Nebraska was once known as "The Bugeaters' State."

In 1895 the Nebraska Legislature voted to call Nebraska "The Tree-Planters' State."

Then, in 1945, the Legislature adopted the name, "The Cornhusker State."

Chapter 17:
The Town-Builders

When Nebraska Territory was formed in 1854, the town-builders were the first pioneers to move into the new land.

The town-builders crossed the Missouri River and began to lay out their towns. The new towns grew rapidly. Nebraska City, which you see in this old drawing, became an important town in pioneer Nebraska.

This is Brownville in 1881. Brownville was one of the first towns built in Nebraska Territory.

Indians who still lived on the land watched in amazement as the new towns were built. What do you think the Indians thought about the white mens' towns?

The town-builders were full of energy and enthusiasm. They all believed that their towns would be successful. The town-builders were sure that they would make a great deal of money in Nebraska Territory.

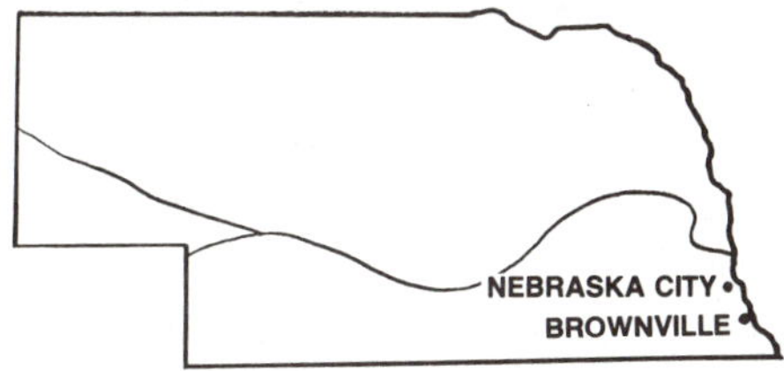

How did the town-builders go about making their towns in Nebraska Territory?

The first step was for men to discover the opportunities that awaited them in Nebraska.

For example, John MacMurphy lived in New York City. One day MacMurphy read an article about Nebraska. He talked to his friends, and they all decided to come to Nebraska and build a town.

Mr. MacMurphy later said, "We were certain that if we would only go to Nebraska in the spring we would in a short space of time become very wealthy."

So he and his friends came to Nebraska and helped build the town of Decatur.

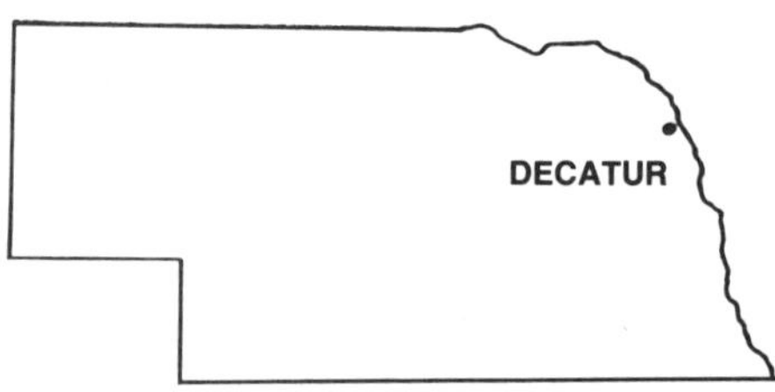

Mr. MacMurphy helped build this new town in Nebraska Territory.

The next step was for the men who wanted to build a town to form a town company. Mr. MacMurphy called his town company The New York Company.

The members of the company elected officers and decided where the town would be built.

Of course, town-building took money. Men who invested money in the company received a piece of paper like this. It was called a stock certificate.

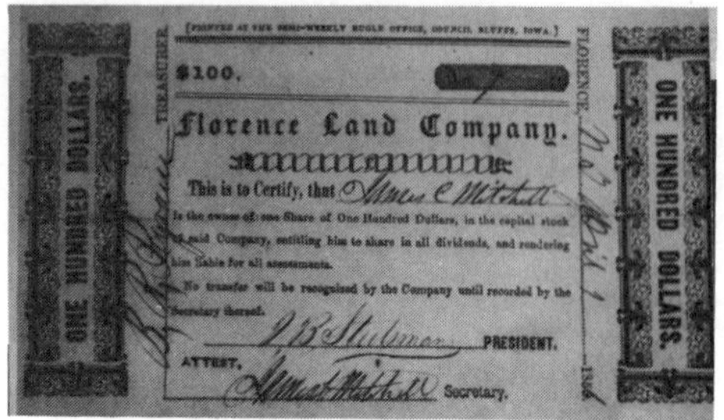
ONE HUNDRED DOLLARS.

TREASURER.

$100.

Florence Land Company.

This is to Certify, that

PRESIDENT.

ATTEST,

Secretary.

FLORENCE,

ONE HUNDRED DOLLARS.

This stock certificate was issued by the company that laid out the town of Florence. Florence now is a part of north Omaha.

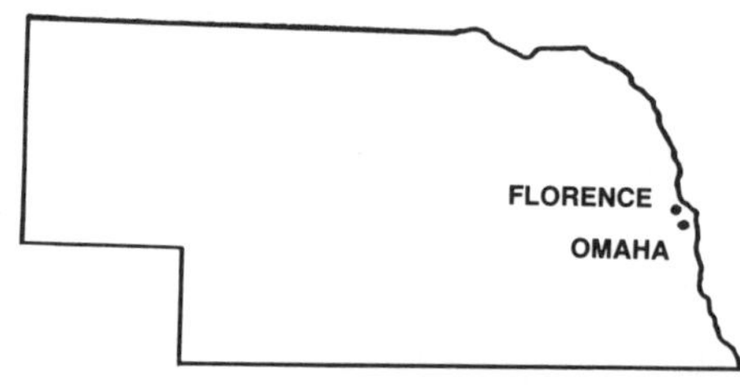

These town companies were very interesting. One company was formed by German immigrants who lived in Davenport, Iowa. They selected a spot along the Platte River for their town, and they named it Grand Island. These German town-builders hoped that one day their town would become the capital of the United States.

A town company made up of

men from Des Moines, Iowa, laid out the town of Fremont.

Table Rock, in southeastern Nebraska, was built by C. W. Giddings and members of a town company who came from Pennsylvania.

The history of one Nebraska town company begins on a steamboat which got stuck in the Missouri River. During the time the boat was stuck, men on board formed a town company, elected officers and even adopted a name for the town they planned to build in Nebraska. The town was named Beatrice, for the daughter of one of the town builders.

Don't you wonder about the men and women who built your town? Where do you suppose they came from?

There are men and women in your People Bank who can tell you about your town and its town-builders. Go talk to these people.

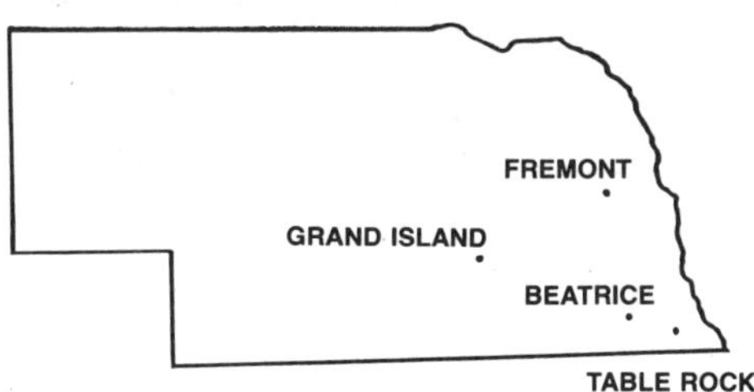

Now that the town-builders had formed their town companies, the next step was to find the best places to build their towns.

The first towns in Nebraska Territory were all laid out along the Missouri River. The town-builders wanted steamboats to be able to bring passengers right to their towns.

They also selected places where there were many trees which could be used for fuel and lumber.

The town-builders also tried to build their towns near the covered wagon trails. They knew that the town would get a lot of business from the people who went west in their covered wagons.

After selecting good places for their towns, the town-builders began to advertise their towns.

Omaha's builders printed a map of their new city. The maps had to be printed in St. Louis. There wasn't a print shop in Omaha yet.

Hundreds of the maps were handed out to persons traveling on the Missouri River steamboats. The Omaha town-builders hoped some of the people would decide to settle in Omaha.

Study this drawing very carefully. It shows people getting off a steamboat at Omaha.

What is going on in the picture? What do you suppose the people are talking about?

"Step ashore, ladies and gentlemen. Welcome to Omaha City. Yes, indeed, welcome to Omaha City, destined to be the finest, the greatest city in the Missouri valley. Step up and get your free map of our city. Promise to build a house and we'll give you a lot, absolutely free! Just think — a free lot that in a few months will be worth thousands of dollars. Yes, ladies and gentlemen, your future is here, in Omaha City!"

Of course, the new towns had to have buildings. One of the first buildings put up was a hotel. Visitors would stay in the hotel while they looked over the town.

This is the Brownville House, a hotel in pioneer Brownville. It was one of the best-known hotels in Nebraska Territory — good food and clean beds.

There were stores to be built, too. J. L. Carson's bank and John Ponn's dry goods and grocery store also stood in the lively town of Brownville.

One of the town's most important businesses was the newspaper. Look carefully at this photograph of downtown Omaha back in pioneer days.

See the building on the corner? That is the office of the Omaha *Herald,* an important pioneer newspaper.

Like all newspapers at this time, the *Herald* was filled with information about the new town of Omaha. Copies of the newspaper were sent all over the country. It was by reading these newspapers that many Eastern people learned about Nebraska's towns.

The town-builders laid out many towns along the Missouri River. Some of the towns did very well. They grew and prospered. Other towns disappeared after a few years.

Look at the map below. It shows some of the towns that were built along the Missouri River. Now, take a map of modern Nebraska. What towns have disappeared from the Nebraska map?

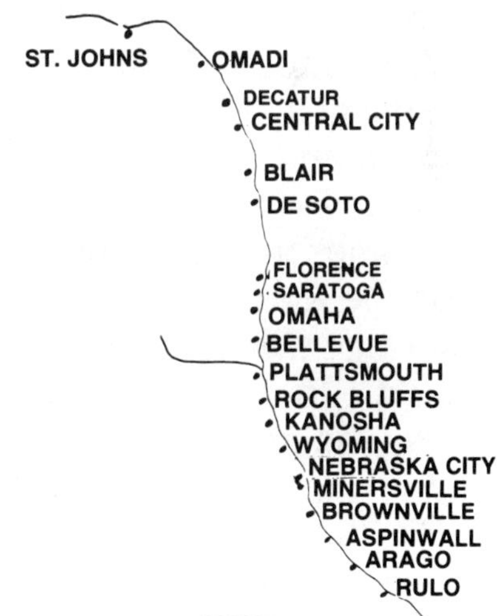

As the years passed town-builders began to build new towns on the western prairies. This map shows you Franklin County, which is in the Republican River country in southwestern Nebraska.

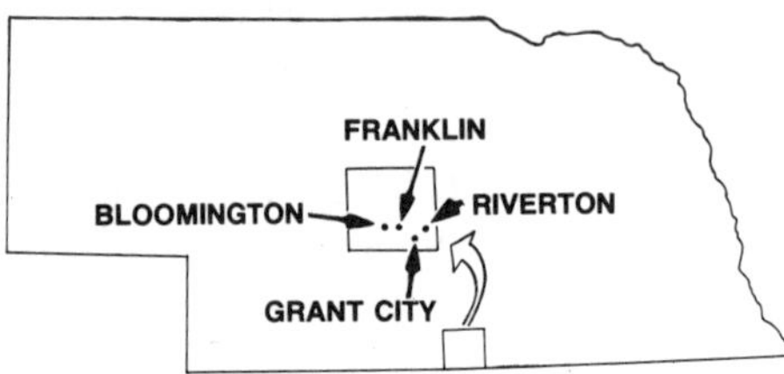

In the 1870's town-builders established the four towns you see on the map.

Bloomington was laid out by town-builders who came from Brownville. Another town company, made up of men who lived in Plattsmouth, built the town of Franklin.

J. W. Thompson formed a town company in Omaha. Thompson and his friends built the town of Riverton. By the way, Thompson Creek flows through the town.

Grant City was laid out by another group of Omaha town-builders. The men who belonged to this town company were Black pioneers. Unfortunately, Grant City did not prosper, and the Black town-builders returned to Omaha.

John Cozad founded a town in Dawson County. It was named for Cozad, the town-builder.

Mr. Cozad printed posters, like the one you see above, and put them up in Cincinnati, Ohio. He invited his friends in Ohio to visit his new town in Nebraska.

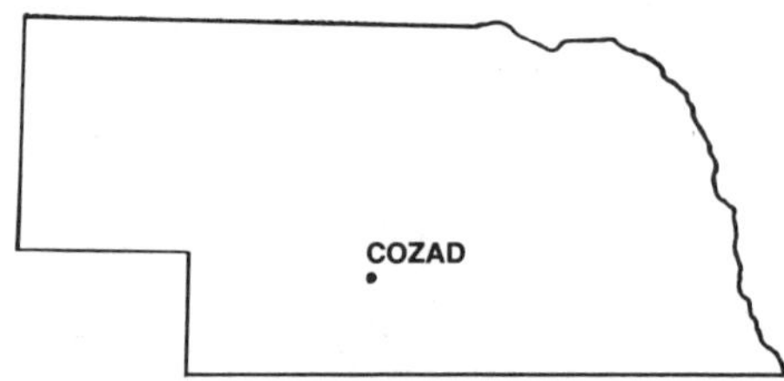

What would a visitor find in these new Nebraska towns?

Certainly, the visitor would find a newspaper office. Every

town had a newspaper, some times more than one.

Usually there was a land office in the town. At this McCook land office, settlers could buy the land they needed for their homes and for their farms.

And when it came time to build houses, barns and stores, the lumber yard did a good business in the new town.

The livery stable was a very busy place. If you wanted to look around the country, you came here to rent a horse and buggy.

At the blacksmith shop you would have shoes put on your horses and repairs made to your wagons and buggies. The blacksmith shop was the town's service station back in horse and buggy days.

Many pioneer towns were built near rivers. Dams were built across the river, and water power was generated to power mills. This is the mill at Neligh. Farmers brought their grain to these mills to be made into flour and feed.

Other town-builders tried to find coal. A few mines opened in eastern Nebraska. This one was near Brownville. But the town-builders never found much coal. But isn't it interesting that more than a hundred years ago the Nebraska town-builders knew how important it was to have a supply of cheap energy? The pioneers thought about energy a great deal.

The town-builders tried very hard to get factories for their towns. Factories provided jobs for the men who came to live in the new towns.

The men who built West Point did a good job in attracting and building industries. The town-builders raised money and helped build several factories in the town.

West Point also had a paper mill, a furniture factory, a creamery and a brick factory.

There was even a soda pop factory, which you see in this old photograph.

This is the West Point flour mill.

West Point soon became one of the busiest and most successful towns in Nebraska.

Life in Nebraska's prairie towns was interesting, and often very exciting. On the Fourth of July everyone turned out to see the big parade.

Baseball was the favorite sport in town. One summer day in 1871 the Milford Blue Belts defeated the Seward team, 97 to 25. The Milford boys were pleased with their victory over their neighbors to the north.

In winter there were plays and programs to attend at the town's Opera House.

The highlight of the summer came with the chautauqua. Families camped out on the chautauqa grounds and spent their time attending meetings and listening to famous speakers.

Men spent at least one evening every week attending lodge meetings. These men belonged to a lodge known as the Modern Woodmen of the World. This is how they dressed for their meetings and programs.

A very important group of men in town were the men who had served in the Union Army during the Civil War. These old veterans always led the parades on Memorial Day and the Fourth of July. They had many, many interesting stories to pass on to the boys in town.

It was fun to stand on the street of a prairie town and watch the people who had come to town to shop.

It was fun to go into the store and to look over the goods that were for sale.

It was fun to visit the big, new bank building. This was quite a building — all brick and fire-proof. The building showed that the town of Albion was really becoming an important place.

And it was really fun to live in a town, such as Lincoln, where you could ride in trolley cars pulled by mules.

The town-builders wanted their towns to be good places for families to live. They were proud of the comfortable homes that lay along the dirt streets.

The town-builders also helped build modern school houses, like this one in West Point.

And they hired good teachers to help the attentive children learn their lessons.

Of course, in every town there were churches where the people met to worship.

Yes, pioneer towns were very busy places. But do you know what? Back in the 1880's, just about a hundred years ago, children who lived in Oakdale complained to the editor of the newspaper. They said that they were bored — there was nothing for them to do in town.

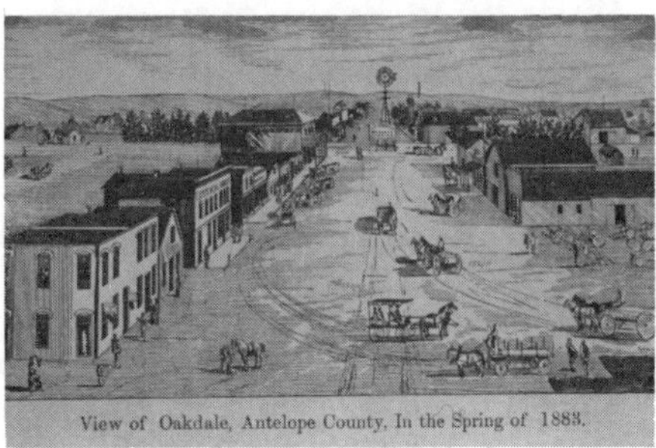

View of Oakdale, Antelope County, In the Spring of 1883.

"Yes, the town-builders were very, very important Nebraska pioneers."

"Now let's find out about the people who built the town or city where you live!"

1. What is the name of your town or city?
2. How did your community get its name?
3. Do some of the streets in your town have interesting names? How did these streets get their names?
4. Where is your town located? Why do you suppose the town-builders selected this spot for a town?
5. What were the names of the early town-builders who came to your community?
6. Where did these town-builders come from?
7. Why do you suppose they wanted to build a town?
8. Now, look carefully at the buildings in your community. Do any of the buildings have names and dates written on them? Find out about these names and dates.

As you find the answers to these questions you will be discovering the story of the community where you live.

Another thing: go to your People Bank and find some person who will take you on a tour of your cemetery. I'm sure that in the cemetery you will find the graves of many town-builders.

And make certain you visit with the men and women, from your People Bank, who can tell you stories about the town or city where you live.

Heritage Special

There is history in the names of streets.

See what the street names in downtown Omaha tell us about the past!

Capitol Avenue	The territorial capitol building of Nebraska was located on this street. Central High School now stands on that site.
Dodge Street	Augustus C. Dodge was a United States Senator from Iowa. He helped write the law which set up Nebraska Territory in 1854.
Douglas Street	Stephen A. Douglas, United States Senator from Illinois, also supported the law which created Nebraska Territory.
Farnam Street	Henry Farnam was an eastern banker and railroad builder. He owned the Chicago and Rock Island Railroad, one of the first railroads to reach the Missouri River.
Harney Street	In 1855 General W. S. Harney led soldiers into western Nebraska and fought a battle with the Sioux Indians. You read about him in Chapter 16.
Howard Street	T. P. Howard was with the Lewis and Clark expedition.
Jackson Street	This street was named for President Andrew Jackson. Jackson was the leader of the Democratic party. Many of Omaha's town-builders were also Democrats.

There Is History In City and Town Names

Wisner...was named for Samuel P. Wisner, who was an officer of the railroad that laid out the town.

Neligh...named for John Neligh a very important Nebraska town-builder. He was also the founder of West Point.

Magnet...a town in Cedar County, it was named Magnet in the hope that the town would attract settlers the way a magnet attracts pieces of iron.

Wynot...another town in Cedar County. Some person in the new town said, "Why not name the town Wynot?"

Valentine...is the county seat of Cherry County, and it is named for E. K. Valentine, who represented Nebraska in the United States Congress for six years.

Allen...in Dixon County, was named for Henry Allen who in 1870 homesteaded the land on which the town was later built.

O'Neill...is named for General John O'Neill, who brought Irish immigrants to live in the community.

Springview is in Keya Paha County. It is said that the town was named for a spring that used to flow near the town. It is also said that one of the first settlers, John F. Carr, hauled water and kept the spring running while visitors were in town. Once the town was located, no water has come from the spring.

A Fun Thing To Do

Go to your People Bank and find persons who can tell you about the history of your county. Ask them to tell you about the towns that have disappeared from the county map. On a map of your county put in the names of these "ghost towns."

See if you can discover the reasons why towns die and disappear.

Omaha: History in Photographs

This is how downtown Omaha looked in the 1860's. The photo was taken on Farnam Street.

The most famous hotel in Omaha was the Herndon House. Notice the stage coaches in the street. People boarded stages for California at the Herndon House.

The J.A. Ware Bank stood at the corner of 17th and Farnam. Notice how the people are dressed.

Omaha high school was built on Capitol Hill, overlooking the city.

These young ladies graduated from Omaha High School in 1876.

Residents of Omaha used street cars to get to work.

This is Omaha in 1916. Look at the old cars. Those are street car tracks running down the street.

Chapter 18:
Political Pioneers

This is J. Sterling Morton, a well-known and important political leader of Nebraska. He was also the founder of Arbor Day, the day when we plant trees in Nebraska.

Mr. Morton was born in New York and grew up in Michigan. He was an ambitious young man, and in 1854 he decided to come to Nebraska Territory. He wanted to become a successful businessman, and he also wanted to be a politician.

There were many other young men back east, just like Mr. Morton. And they also decided to come to Nebraska. In the new Territory of Nebraska there were many opportunities for men who wanted to be political pioneers.

Territorial Government

Francis Burt was sent by Congress to be the first governor of Nebraska Territory.

He came by steamboat to Bellevue. Fifteen persons stood at the edge of the Missouri River to greet the new governor when he stepped off the boat. (These fifteen persons were just about the entire population of Bellevue in 1854.)

On every person's mind was the question, what city will Governor Burt choose to be the capital of Nebraska Territory?

The town that was named capital would have a wonderful chance to grow and prosper. In fact, the capital city would probably become the largest and most important city in Nebraska.

Governor Burt probably wanted to make Bellevue the capital city; but Mr. Burt died a few days after he arrived in Nebraska.

Thomas Cuming then became acting or temporary governor, and he decided that the capital would be located in Omaha.

The first session of the territorial legislature met in this little brick building in Omaha.

Later a larger capitol building was erected on a hill overlooking the new city of Omaha.

Mark Izard was named to be the second governor of Nebraska Territory. He arrived in Omaha in January, 1855. The weather was very cold.

The folks in Omaha decided that they would have a dance and dinner to welcome Mr. Izard.

The City Hotel, a rough, wooden building at the corner of Harney and Eleventh Streets was chosen for the party. The building had a wooden floor, and during the afternoon the floor was thoroughly scrubbed with soap and water.

But, you must remember that this happened in January, and the City Hotel was not well heated. So, the water froze on the floor.

Governor Izard arrived at seven o'clock. He was greeted by a large crowd of men and seven women — all the women there were in the city of Omaha at this time.

The band, made up of one fellow who played the violin, began to play. The men and women started to dance, and several women slipped and fell flat on the ice-covered floor.

At midnight the people stopped for supper. They had black coffee, slices of meat on dark bread and dried apple pie.

The men elected by the settlers to serve in the territorial legislature had many important jobs to do. First, they had to write laws for the territory. Then they had to provide a system of courts and judges. They also had to set taxes and collect money to run the government.

Of course, the legislators did not always agree on everything. There were many arguments among the legislators. Representatives who came from south of the Platte River usually fought with the men who lived on the north side of the Platte River. These were really the first two political parties in Nebraska — the "South Platters" against the "North Platters."

County Government

The territorial law-makers laid out counties and ordered elections held for county officials. The men who took over these county jobs had many important things to do also.

County officers had to see that roads were built and cared for. They had to see that schools opened and school taxes collected.

The counties also took care of poor people, and the county sheriffs were important law officers.

When a county was formed by the legislature, the big question was where the county seat of the county would be located.

The county seat, as you know, is the town where the county court house and county offices are located. Having the county seat gave a town a great advantage over other towns. Many people went to the county seat on business. This meant that they would do their shopping in the county seat town too.

In many Nebraska counties towns fought one another to get the county seat. The people of the county voted on which town they wanted for the county seat. But it was not unusual for these elections to be dishonest. Several elections were often held before the matter was settled.

Lowell court house

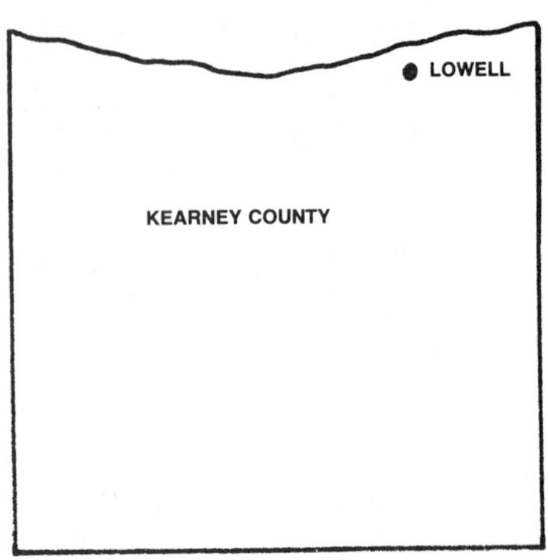

The town of Lowell was the first county seat of Kearney County. The county used tax money to build a fine brick courthouse in Lowell.

However, as you can see on the map, Lowell was way up the northeastern corner of the county. People in the west end of the county had a long trip to the county seat.

Joel Hull

Joel Hull lived on a farm near the center of the county. He and some of his neighbors decided that the county seat should be moved from Lowell to a spot near the center of the county. Lowell and his friends said they would build a town at the center of the county if the voters agreed to move the county seat. The new town was to be named Minden.

An election was held, and Lowell lost the county seat. Of course, there was no town of Minden as yet. The county officers said there was no money to build the new town; so Hull set up a town company. His company built the new town of Minden. It even paid for a new court house.

Look carefully at this photograph. What do you suppose is happening?

Well, that is the Box Butte county court house on the railroad car.

For years the court house was located in the town of Hemingford. Then the voters decided to move the county seat to Alliance.

So the wooden court house was loaded on a railroad car and carried to Alliance, the new county seat.

What about your county? Was there a fight over the county seat in your county? Find some one in your People Bank who can tell you the story of your county seat.

Town Government

The new prairie towns also needed governments. The settlers in the towns elected men to serve in office. These men then had to write laws that bring law and order to the new towns.

One of the first laws passed in Lincoln made it against the law for a person to let his hogs run loose in the streets.

Columbus had a problem with young men who raced their horses up and down the main street. So, the town leaders had a big ditch dug across the street. They hoped this would slow down the daring young men on their fast horses.

Many towns had laws that said baseball could not be played on Sundays. There were also laws against dancing and having parties on Sundays.

There were curfews in prairie towns. A curfew is a law that says all young people have to be off the streets and in their homes by a certain time.

Towns passed laws dealing with stoves and chimneys. Remember that almost all of the houses and stores in the towns were made of wood. Fire was a real problem. More than one town in Nebraska was almost completely destroyed by fires. The first policemen hired by the towns spent most of their time watching for fires.

Towns also set up fire departments. In the early days of the town, people donated money so that fire-fighting equipment could be bought. But as the towns grew larger, tax money was used to buy fire engines and to train firemen.

One other thing about fires. Nebraska towns had to be protected against prairie fires. In the fall when the grass became very dry, men plowed "fire guards" around the town.

They plowed the ground in order to turn the dry grass under. Then a prairie fire would burn up to the fire guard and stop. Prairie fires were a real danger to early Nebraska towns.

State Government

As the years passed more and more people moved to Nebraska. In 1867 Nebraska was ready to become a state.

On March 1, 1869, President Andrew Johnson signed the bill that created the State of Nebraska.

Nebraska's law-makers decided to move the capital from Omaha. Three men were appointed by the legislature to find a good place for the state capital.

These men looked over several places, and they told the legislators that the best place was at the town of Lancaster in Lancaster County.

The legislators accepted the idea, and Lancaster, which was renamed Lincoln, became the capital of the new State of Nebraska.

This is the first state capitol building in Lincoln.

Here is the second state capitol building.

Here is Nebraska's third capitol building.

"Now you know how important the political pioneers were in building Nebraska. State, county and town offices were filled by persons who wanted to serve the people."

Special Nebraskans

Robert Furnas

Robert Furnas was born in Ohio. Both of his parents died when he was eight years old. As a boy he worked in a grocery store and for a tinsmith. He never attended school. He gained his education through experience and by teaching himself. Finally he became a printer and ran a newspaper.

In 1856 he came to Brownville, Nebraska Territory, where he edited a local newspaper. Mr. Furnas was a real town-builder. He worked hard to help Brownville develop.

He was also interested in Nebraska. He was a real supporter of farmers. And he published a newspaper, *The Nebraska Farmer,* which helped the farmers understand their land.

In 1872 he was elected the second governor of the State of Nebraska.

R. W. Furnas as governor

William Jennings Bryan:

Mr. Bryan was a very important politician. After serving in the United States House of Representatives, Mr. Bryan three times was nominated by the Democratic party for the office of President. Mr. Bryan was known as "The Great Commoner," because he always tried to speak for the common people of Nebraska and the nation.

William Jennings Bryan

George W. Norris:

George Norris was born in Ohio. He came to Nebraska in 1885 as a lawyer. He lived first in Beaver City. Then he moved to McCook.

Mr. Norris was elected to the House of Representatives, and in 1910 he was elected to the United States Senate. Mr. Norris was particularly interested in finding ways to provide cheap electricity to the people, especially the farm families of Nebraska.

For forty years Mr. Norris was one of America's best-known political leaders.

You can visit his home in McCook. It is a State museum.

License Plate History

6-1486	Number 6 county is Saunders County which is named for Alvin Saunders, a territorial governor. He also served as a United States senator from Nebraska.
19-4683	Richardson County, number 19 county, is named for another territorial governor, William A. Richardson.
24-1990	Cuming County is named for Thomas Cuming who served as acting governor after Mr. Burt died.
25-1204	Butler County is named for David Butler, the first governor of the State of Nebraska.

The State Seal of Nebraska

Every State has a seal which tells about the State. Below you can see the State Seal of Nebraska. This Seal also appears on our State flag.

1. What is Nebraska's official slogan?
2. What is the man doing who is pictured on the Seal? Why was this kind of worker used on the Seal?
3. What kinds of transportation do you see?
4. How do you know, by looking at the Seal, that there are farms in Nebraska?
5. What is the meaning of the date, March 1, 1867?
6. Look carefully at the Seal: What kind of place is Nebraska?

Lincoln: Nebraska's Capital City

Lincoln in the 1860's.

Lincoln in 1872. This photo, taken from the top of the capitol building, shows the University of Nebraska building at the north edge of town. How many trees do you see in the picture?

O Street in the 1880's.

O Street in the 1920's. Notice the automobiles and the streetcars.

O Street today.

What do you think O Street will look like when your children are in school studying Nebraska history?

Chapter 19:
Rails West!

Do you remember how the first pioneers traveled to Nebraska?

Many rode horses. There were some who walked. And there were those who came in wagons pulled by horses, mules and oxen. Then, the steamboat was invented, and thousands of town-builders and political pioneers came to Nebraska on those boats that used the Missouri River.

By the time Nebraska Territory was formed in 1854, however, just about all the pioneers were talking about the railroad.

Iron rails had been laid in many Eastern states, and steam engines were pulling railroad cars over those rails.

People could hardly believe the stories they heard about the railroad. Railroad trains went as fast as fifteen miles an hour! And they didn't get stuck in the mud!

To the prairie pioneers the railroads were like a dream come true. Imagine being able to travel quickly and easily over the prairie.

In 1862 the United States Congress passed a law which said that a railroad would be built from the Missouri River to the Pacific Ocean.

Many people laughed at the idea of building a railroad across the plains and the mountains. They said that it just couldn't be done.

The Union Pacific Railroad company began to build the railroad west from Omaha. The men who owned the Union Pacific Railroad had trouble getting the money they needed to build the railroad.

The United States government helped out by giving to the

railroad millions of acres of land. The railroad company sold the land and used the money to pay for the railroad.

Once work started on the railroad, Omaha became a busy place. Most of the materials needed to build the railroad had to be brought by steamboat up the Missouri.

The railroad company also had to hire hundreds of men to lay the track.

Soon everything was ready for work to begin. Workers began laying the iron rails across the plains. Look at this old drawing carefully:

BUILDING THE UNION PACIFIC RAILROAD IN NEBRASKA. PAGE 567

Can you hear the boss calling out his orders? Can you hear the hammers pounding the spikes into the wooden ties?

And this went on, mile after mile, as the Union Pacific Railroad was built across Nebraska.

The Union Pacific Railroad started in Omaha. It followed the Platte Valley across eastern and central Nebraska. It then crossed the prairies into Wyoming.

Here is where the Union Pacific began in Omaha. The gentlemen wearing the top hats are officials with the railroad who came to see how the work was going.

As the Union Pacific moved west, towns grew up along the new tracks.

The town-builders who laid out Columbus knew how important the railroad was to their town. So they put the town right next to the track.

The workers laid more than a thousand miles of track west from Omaha. Then, on May 10, 1869, the Union Pacific met the Central Pacific, the railroad that was being built east from California.

There was a big celebration when the two railroads met. The transcontinental railroad was completed!

Now a person could get on a train in Omaha and in several days arrive in California. A trip that had taken months in a covered wagon could now be taken in just days.

Just think of the change! In the 1840's people crossed the plains in prairie schooners. Thirty years later, they traveled swiftly and comfortably in a railroad car.

A few years later another important railroad was built in Nebraska. This was the Burlington and Missouri Railroad. Tracks of the Burlington were laid from Plattsmouth to Kearney. Then the railroad built through southwestern Nebraska and on to Denver.

Clarks, in Merrick County, was named for S. H. Clark, an official of the Union Pacific Railroad.

Benedict, in York County, was named for E. C. Benedict, president of the Kansas City and Omaha Railroad.

Sidney, in Cheyenne County, was named for Sidney Dillon, an officer with the Union Pacific Railroad.

Blair, in Washington County, was named for John Blair, an important railroad builder in Illinois, Iowa and Nebraska.

In the 1870's a Nebraska newspaper editor wrote, "Nebraska has caught a bad case of railroad fever!"

He was right. Every Nebraska town-builder wanted a railroad built to his town. All over Nebraska people were talking about railroads! Railroads would bring prosperity to Nebraska!

The railroad companies often asked towns and counties for money. After all, said the railroad companies, it cost a great deal of money to build railroads. The towns and counties should help pay for building the railroads.

So the people in the towns and counties voted bonds for the railroads. The money from the bonds was given to the railroads. The people then paid taxes for many years in order to pay off the bonds.

Brownville

This is Brownville. In the 1870's it was a very successful town, as you can see by the photograph. Brownville's citizens voted thousands of dollars in bonds to build a railroad. But the men who ran the railroad company were crooks. They took Brownville's money but never built the railroad.

The people who lived in Brownville had to pay for the bonds they had given to the company. Taxes became very, very high; and people moved away from Brownville.

Because of the railroad that was never built, the town of Brownville almost died.

Yes, the railroad meant life or death for a prairie town.

What happened to towns that did not get a railroad? Many towns died. Others, like Brownville, practically disappeared. But some town-builders just moved their stores and houses across the prairie to a new town site along the railroad.

The railroad companies laid out many towns. In this picture you see the prairie town of Benedict in York County. It had been laid out by a railroad company.

The railroads wanted to have stations or depots every eight or ten miles along their tracks. This made it easy for farmers, who used horse-drawn wagons, to bring their crops to the stations. And, of course, usually a little town grew up around the station or depot.

In Nebraska's prairie towns the depot was the busiest and most interesting place in town. The boys in town, in particular, always hung out around the depot. There always seemed to be something going on at the depot.

Adults liked to come to the depot too. They watched the trains come and go. The adults were always interested in seeing who was coming into town and who was leaving.

The merchants in town had to come down to the depot to pick up their goods that came in by train. And the grain merchants and livestock dealers in town shipped their products to market on the railroad.

Yes, the railroad depot was the center of a Nebraska town.

As you know, the Union Pacific Railroad, and also the Burlington, received millions of acres of land from the United States government.

The railroads wanted to sell their land to farmers and ranchers. So they printed posters which told people back east about the land that could be bought in Nebraska.

Read this Union Pacific land poster. Why should a person come to Nebraska? What reasons are given on the poster for coming to Nebraska?

RICH FARMING LANDS!

ON THE LINE OF THE

Union Pacific Railroad!

Located in the GREAT CENTRAL BELT of POPULATION, COMMERCE and WEALTH, and adjoining the WORLD'S HIGHWAY from OCEAN TO OCEAN.

12,000,000 ACRES!

3.000,000 Acres in Central and Eastern Nebráska, in the Platte Valley, now for sale!

We invite the attention of all parties seeking a HOME, to the LANDS offered for sale by this Company.

The Vast Quantity of Land from which to select, enables every one to secure such a location as he desires, suitable to any branch of farming or stock raising.

The Prices are Extremely Low. The amount of land owned by the Company is so large that they are determined to sell at the cheapest possible rates, ranging from $1.50 to $8.00 per acre.

The Terms of Payment are Easy. Ten years' credit at six per cent interest. A deduction of ten per cent for cash.

The Location is Central, along the 41st parallel, the favorite latitude of America. Equally well adapted to corn or wheat; free from the long, cold winters of the Northern, and the hot, unhealthy influences of the Southern States.

The Face of the Country is diversified with hill and dale, grain land and meadow, rich bottoms, low bluffs, and undulating tables, all covered with a thick growth of sweet nutritious grasses.

The Soil is a dark loam, slightly impregnated with lime, free from stone and gravel, and eminently adapted to grass, grain and root crops; the subsoil is usually light and porous, retaining moisture with wonderful tenacity.

The Climate is mild and healthful; the atmosphere dry and pure. Epidemic diseases never prevail; Fever and Ague are unknown. The greatest amount of rain falls between March and October. The Winters are dry with but little snow.

The Productions are wheat, corn, oats, barley, rye and root crops, and vegetables generally. Flax, sweet potatoes, sorghum, etc., etc., do well and yield largely.

Fruits, both Wild and Cultivated, do remarkably well, The freedom from frosts in May and September, in connection with the dry Winters and warm soil, renders this State eminently adapted to fruit culture.

Stock Raising in all its branches, is particularly profitable on the wide ranges of rich pasturage. Cattle and sheep feed with avidity and fatten upon the nutritious grasses without grain; hogs thrive well, and wool growing is exceedingly remunerative.

Timber is found on the streams and grows rapidly.

Coal of excellent quality, exists in vast quantities on the line of the road in Wyoming, and is furnished to settlers at reduced rates.

Market Facilities are the best in the West; the great mining regions of Wyoming, Colorado, Utah and Nevada, are supplied by the farmers of Platte Valley.

The Title given the purchaser is absolute, in fee simple, and free from all incumbrances, derived directly from the United States.

Soldiers of the Late War are entitled to a Homestead of one hundred and sixy acres, within Railroad limits, which is equal to a bounty of $400.

Persons of Foreign Birth are also entitled to the benefits of the Free Homestead Law, on declaring their intentions of becoming citizens of the United States; this they may do immediately on their arrival in this country.

For Colonies, the lands on the line of the Union Pacific Railroad afford the *best locations* in the West.

TOWN LOTS FOR SALE VERY CHEAP in the most important towns on the line of the Road, affording excellent opportunities for business or investments.

Full information in regard to lands, prices, terms of sale, &c., together with pamphlets, circulars and maps, may be obtained from all the Agents of the Department, also the

"PIONEER."

A handsome ILLUSTRATED PAPER, with maps, etc., and containing the HOMESTEAD LAW. *Mailed free* to all applicants. Address

O. F. DAVIS,
Land Commissioner, U. P. R. R.
OMAHA, NEB.

What was it like to ride on a pioneer railroad train?

Traveling on these first trains was exciting, but not very comfortable.

The passengers sat on hard wooden benches. On hot summer days the windows were wide open. Smoke, soot and sparks poured in upon the passengers.

At night flickering candles or a few kerosene lanterns provided a little light. During the winter the people in the cars were always cold. A small coal-burning stove at one end of the car could not keep the people warm.

Eating was a problem. Many people carried food with them. Other passengers jumped from the cars when the train stopped at a depot. Most depots had an "eating house" where passengers could buy a meal. Usually the train stopped for twenty or thirty minutes so the passengers could eat.

Since the tracks were rough, the cars bounced and swayed from side to side. Although the trains went slowly — fifteen or twenty miles an hour was the top speed for passenger trains — the passengers in the cars were frequently bounced from their seats.

The railroad cars were fastened together with chains. Railroad workers had to fasten the cars together with these chains. It was dangerous work. Many workers lost fingers and hands in accidents.

Brakes on the trains were operated by hand. Each car had its own set of brakes, and these brakes were operated by brakemen who rode on the top of the cars. Whenever the engineer signalled with his whistle that he needed brakes, the brakemen quickly turned the wheel on top of the car that applied the brakes. Then the brakemen ran along the top of the car to the next car, where he quickly turned the wheel.

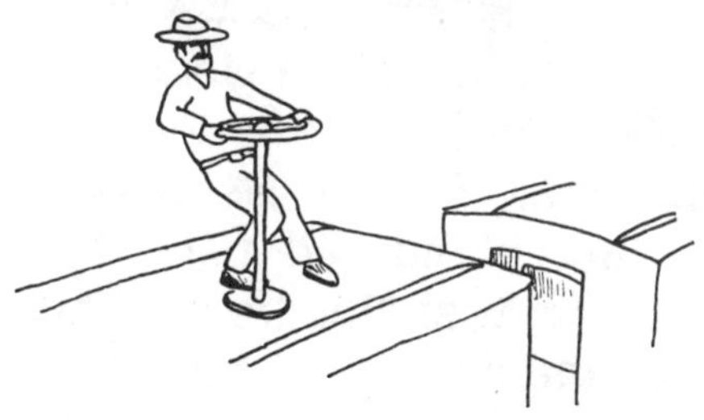

Brakemen performed this job night and day, in all kinds of weather. It would be hard to think of a more dangerous job.

The truth is, the pioneer railroaders faced danger constantly.

There were many collisions between trains.

Heavy rains would wash out tracks and destroy bridges, and the trains would plunge off the tracks. Blizzards buried trains on the prairie.

One day in 1877 a Union Pacific train stopped at the depot at Big Springs, Nebraska.

A band of masked men leaped on board the train. They forced the men in the baggage car to open the safe. The train robbers dashed off with about $60,000 in gold coins.

Sam Bass was a member of this gang. He escaped to Texas with his share of the money. All of the other train robbers were caught. But it wasn't long before Sam Bass was shot and killed during a bank holdup in Texas.

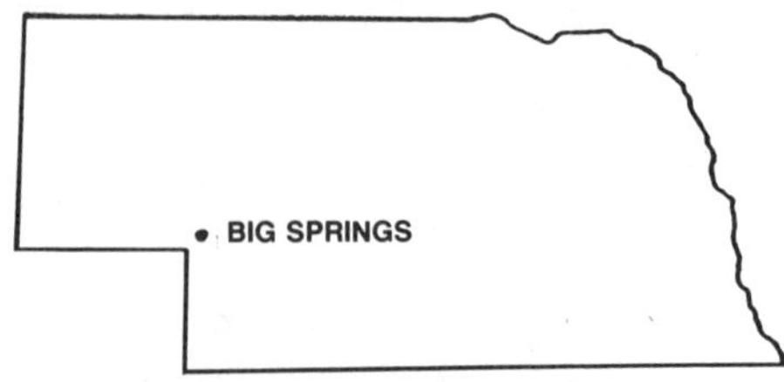

Sam Bass

What do you suppose the Indians thought about the railroad trains?

At first the Indians were very curious about the smoke-belching, snorting engines. But before long they began to hate the railroad. They knew that the railroad trains brought more and more white people to fill up the land.

Angry Indians often attacked the workers as they laid the track. In western Nebraska the workers kept their rifles close at hand. They knew the Indians were always near; the workers had to be ready to fight off an attack at any time.

Some Pawnee Scouts

At this time a man by the name of Frank North lived in Columbus. North had lived among the Pawnee Indians. He spoke the Pawnee language and he had many friends among the Pawnee.

North asked some of the Pawnee men to join the Army. North would be their commander. This group was known as the Pawnee Scouts. One of their main jobs was that of protecting the workers on the railroad.

In August, 1867, Cheyenne Indians led by Chief Turkey Leg wrecked a train just west of Lexington. (At this time the town of Lexington was called Plum Creek.)

The Indians killed several members of the train crew. The Indians broke open the freight cars and stole whatever they wanted.

In one car they found bolts of cloth. Grabbing the end of the cloth, the Indians rode their horses as fast as they could over the prairie. The bolts of cloth unrolled behind them. Soon the grass was covered with cloth.

But in a few hours the Pawnee Scouts arrived on the scene. They followed the Indians and drove them out of Nebraska. Turkey Leg and his people never again attacked a train.

There is another interesting story about this Indian attack. It is said that one trainman was wounded by the Indians. He dropped to the ground. Thinking the man was dead, an Indian scalped him.

As the Indian mounted his horse, he dropped the scalp. So, after the Indians left, the wounded man picked up his scalp.

A few days later he arrived in Omaha. He was carrying his scalp in a bucket of water and looking for a doctor who might be able to sew his hair back on his head. An interesting story, right?

The coming of the railroad was one of the most important events in the history of pioneer Nebraska.

The railroads brought thousands of new settlers. The railroads gave the farmers, ranchers and factory owners of Nebraska a fast and cheap way of sending their products to market.

And the railroads brought goods from the East which the prairie pioneers needed.

No wonder we see a railroad train on the Great Seal of Nebraska! Do you remember? Look on page 140 if you have forgotten what the Great Seal looks like.

"The railroad was very important to the prairie pioneers. The railroad helped the people who lived on the land and the people who lived in towns."

"Nebraska was the land where the iron rails reached west across the prairie."

The Railroad and a Nebraska Town

You are looking at the first building in the town of Fairview. The town was located in Red Willow County.

A few years later the railroad came through Red Willow County. Men from the railroad took over Fairview and laid out a new town. It didn't take people long to forget Fairview. The new railroad town prospered.

This is the new town of McCook. You can see that McCook, like many Nebraska towns, grew and became an important town because of the railroad.

McCook today. Do you suppose the railroad is as important to McCook as it was in the past?

Some Very Special Nebraskans

These are the Kilpatrick brothers who lived in Beatrice, Nebraska. They built railroads all over the west. In sixteen years their company laid 3,339 miles of railroad. They were very special Nebraskans. They were pioneer railroad builders.

A HERITAGE SPECIAL

Nebraska's Petticoat Pioneers

"Women are a part of Nebraska's history. In pioneer days, women did many important things.

Women came to pioneer Nebraska with their families. They helped to build our towns, farms and ranches.

Many women settled on their own homesteads. Like these young ladies in Custer County, they wanted land of their own.

In pioneer days women did not have the right to vote in national and state elections. These women in York wanted the right to vote.

Willa Cather was one of America's finest authors. She grew up in Red Cloud. Many of her wonderful books tell the story of Nebraska's prairie pioneers.

Chapter 20:
Sod-Busters

"Many prairie pioneers were farmers. They came to Nebraska so that they might have their very own land to farm."

"The pioneer farmers' first job was to plow the land. Since the land was covered with thick, tough sod, this was not an easy job.

Horses and oxen pulled sharp plows through the sod. This was called "breaking" the sod. After the sod had been broken and turned over by the plows, seeds could be planted in the soft ground."

Because they broke or "busted" the sod, the prairie farmers were called "sod-busters."

Perhaps some of your ancestors came to Nebraska to be farmers. Thousands of pioneers came for just that reason. They wanted to own their own farms.

The men and women who decided to settle in Nebraska could get land in several ways.

They could buy land from the railroads. They could also buy land from the United States government. The State of Nebraska had land for sale too.

After 1863 settlers could get free land from the United States government. The Homestead Law said that any man or woman could have 160 acres of free land. The homesteader had to live on the land for five years. After that the land belonged to the person who had settled on it.

Ten years later Congress passed another law. This law said that a settler could have another 160 acres of free land. The settler had to promise to plant trees on part of the 160 acres. Perhaps one of your pioneer ancestors received a "tree claim" under this law.

The important point to remember is this: pioneer farmers could get their land in different ways. Not all of them homesteaded. Many of them bought their land.

"The pioneer farmers had an important decision to make. They had to decide upon the best way to get their land."

What kind of land did the pioneers want?

Those who settled in eastern Nebraska wanted land which lay along streams. The settlers could get water from the streams. But, more important, trees grew along the streams. The trees could be cut down and used to build log cabins. The wood could also be used for fuel.

In these early days many settlers believed that crops would grow only in the valleys. The prairie land, out of the valleys, was thought to be infertile — not good for raising crops.

The settlers who took a homestead or a timber claim had to go to a government land office. There they had their claims written in the record books.

Here is the United States Land Office which once stood in Bloomington. Today this interesting building is in The Pioneer Village in Minden.

The pioneers were anxious to move onto their land. They started at once to build houses.

In eastern Nebraska many pioneer houses were built of logs. In some places the pioneers found stone that could be used to build houses.

Other settlers lived in dugouts. A dugout is a house made by digging a hole in the ground. A stovepipe in the roof carried off the smoke from the stove. A wooden door kept out the wind and rain.

In central and western Nebraska, where there were very few trees, the pioneers built their houses out of sod.

To build his sod house, a pioneer first plowed up long strips of sod. Then he cut the strips into pieces about two feet long. These pieces were then laid one on top of another, making the walls of the house.

"These men are cutting sod to be used in building a sod house."

To make the roof of the house, a layer of sod was laid over poles and tree branches.

It didn't take long to make a sod house, and it didn't cost much either. One pioneer made a list of the things he had to buy:

1 piece of window glass 8″ x 10″	$1.25
18 feet of lumber for the door	.54
Latch and hinges for the door	.50
Stovepipe for the stove	.30
Nails	.19
Total cost	$2.78

A well-built sod house, or "soddie," made a snug home. The walls were about two feet thick. The walls kept the house cool in summer and warm in winter.

The roof was the only weak part of the house. Usually the roof leaked during storms. In dry weather dirt constantly dropped from the roof. Children would be awakened at night by dirt falling in their faces.

Pioneer mothers worked hard to make the sod houses comfortable. They fought a battle with the dirt. Cloth was hung under the roof to catch the dirt. And they pasted newspapers on the walls. These newspapers were called "homesteaders' wallpaper."

Pioneer children liked to visit their neighbors. While the adults talked, the children would sit and read the newspapers on the wall. This was known as "reading the walls."

No matter what they did, pioneer mothers could not get rid of the fleas and bedbugs that lived in the soddies.

The mothers scrubbed the floor with kerosene. They covered the walls with newspapers.

But nothing worked. The bugs and fleas always returned.

During warm weather the family often slept outside. They just let the bugs and fleas have the house!

Rattlesnakes often visited the houses too. Once in a while a snake fell from the roof — right into the middle of the table where the family was eating.

There are many pioneer stories about snakes crawling into the babies' beds. You can bet that pioneer mothers always had a strong stick or a hoe at hand with which to kill the snakes.

Special: **The Lady from Philadelphia**

Philadelphia is a large city in the state of Pennsylvania. In the 1870's a young lady from that city married a man who wanted to live in Nebraska. She came from a very wealthy family. She always had the best clothing and she lived in a fine, comfortable house.

Her husband brought her to his farm in central Nebraska. Here, this lady from Philadelphia lived in a sod house. On this prairie farm she reared her children.

One night it rained very hard. The dirt roof over the soddie began to leak. She placed the kerosene lamp under a chair so the lamp wouldn't go out.

Then she covered her children who were in bed with a piece of heavy oil cloth. And she sat up all night, holding an umbrella over her sleeping children.

She spent most of the night wondering why she had ever left Philadelphia!

The pioneers needed a supply of good water. At first, water was carried from streams. When they had time, the pioneers dug wells near their houses.

Well-digging was hard and dangerous work. In some parts of Nebraska men had to dig two hundred feet or more to get to water.

Many men were killed as they dug wells. The walls would cave in on them, or they would suffocate because the air became bad in the deep wells.

Now the pioneer family has a house and a well. What else do they need?

Yes, they need a supply of fuel for their stove.

Trees along the stream were soon cut down and used for fuel. Then the pioneers had to drive many, many miles to get a wagon load of firewood.

Settlers who had some money went to town and bought coal. Poor settlers, however, burned whatever they could find.

They burned prairie hay, weeds, corn stalks, buffalo chips and cow chips. The pioneers, you see, had a real energy problem.

This lady lived in Kansas. Like the pioneer women of Nebraska, she picked up cow chips to burn in her stove.

Do you see the little girl in the picture?

In the spring the farmers planted their crops. They sowed wheat, rye, oats, barely and flax on the plowed ground.

Do you know what it means to sow a crop?

Look at this picture. Do you know where this statue is located?

Yes, this statue is on the top of our Capitol building in Lincoln. The statue is called "The Sower," because the man is "sowing" or planting grain.

The sack is filled with seed. The farmer takes a handful of seed. As he walks across the field, he scatters the seed over the ground. This is what is known as "sowing."

Planting corn took more time and work. Corn cannot be sowed. The farmers had to plant the kernels of corn very carefully in the ground. Some times this was done by hand; some farmers used a corn planter like the one you see in this drawing.

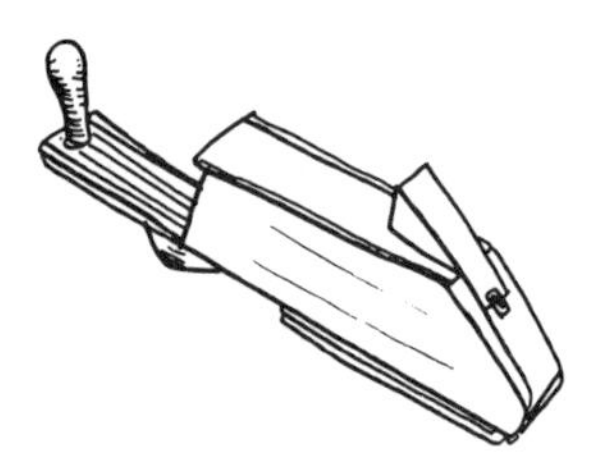

Corn was the pioneers' most important crop. Corn was fed to hogs, cattle and horses. Corn could be burned in the stove. And many dishes the pioneer family ate were made from corn.

Pioneer farmers looked for ways to fence in their fields. They wanted to keep out animals that might trample or eat the growing crops.

Some farmers planted a row of osage orange trees around their fields. These trees grew rapidly. They made a thick hedge that animals could not get through.

Then, barbed wire was invented. Barbed wire really helped the prairie farmers. With this cheap wire, they could fence their land and protect their crops.

During their first years on the land the prairie farmers did not make money.

Some times mothers took jobs in town. One lady, who did housework in town, said she made enough money to feed the horses and her husband.

Men also took extra jobs. Those who had horses and plows could make two or three dollars a day plowing for their neighbors. Men with teams could also find work building railroads.

It was the money from these extra jobs that helped many pioneers stay on their land.

Special: The Cannon Family of Greeley County.

The Cannon family came to Greeley County from Boston,

Massachusetts. Mr. Cannon took some land for a farm. Then he found a job in Grand Island, about fifty miles away from his farm.

Mr. Cannon worked in Grand Island during the week. Then he walked home to be with his family on Sunday.

Mrs. Cannon worked the farm while he was gone. She plowed the ground and planted the crops. At first she walked three miles to a neighbor's farm to get water. Then she dug her own well.

On his way home each week, he stopped at a store in St. Paul and bought a sack of flour. Then he carried the fifty pound sack twenty-seven miles farther to his home.

One time a neighbor walked to Grand Island with Mr. Cannon. The neighbor wanted to buy a stove in Grand Island. The man bought the stove he wanted, lifted it on his back — and walked home fifty miles!

The pioneers did not have much money for clothing. Everyone in the family usually went barefoot in the summer.

One pioneer in Central Nebraska wore out all the clothes he had brought with him from the East. So he made a hat from grass. He tied pads of grass to his feet with leather strings. And he made a pair of pants out of an old sack.

The first settlers feared the Indians. It is easy to understand why. Hostile Indians raided farms. They drove off animals, burned crops and murdered the settlers.

But there were few Indian raids in Nebraska at this time. But there were many Indians still around. They wandered over the country, stopping at farms to ask for food.

Just imagine: a pioneer mother would be working in her sod house. She would look up and find a dozen or more Indians standing silently in the doorway. You can bet she was frightened!

The Indians would make signs that they wanted bread to eat. So the mother would quickly bake some bread or biscuits. She might use up all the flour in the house; but she wanted to feed the Indians so they would leave.

Most of the time the pioneer families had enough to eat. At every meal, however, they ate the same food. They had many dishes made from corn, bread and salt or dried meat.

In summer, of course, they would have vegetables from their gardens. That was a welcome change. The men would also shoot prairie chickens and bring home fresh meat for the table.

The children had fun gathering wild fruit and berries.

Illness was a real problem for the prairie pioneers. They did not have medicines to give to those who were ill. Most of the time they could not get to a doctor either.

Pioneer mothers usually had some home-made medicines on hand. A mixture of onion juice and turpentine, for example, was used to stop coughs.

The pioneers seemed to have one rule about medicines: the worse the medicine tasted, the better it was for you.

Blizzards brought great hardships to the prairie pioneers.

On Easter Sunday, 1873, a terrible blizzard swept across Nebraska. In York County a boy went to the barn to get a sack of corn. He lost his way between the house and the barn and froze to death in the storm.

During that blizzard many families brought their livestock into their sod houses. One family in Seward County lived for three days with four hogs, two cows and thirty chickens in their tiny sod house.

In January, 1888, another blizzard hit Nebraska. This blizzard howled across the land in the afternoon just as children were going home from school. Many children died in the blizzard. So it is often called "The Schoolchildrens' Blizzard."

Etta Shattuck taught a country school in Holt County. After getting all her students home safely, Etta started for her house. She became lost in the storm.

She crawled into a haystack where she lay for three days. Finally, she was found and taken to safety. Her feet were badly frozen, and a few weeks later she died.

Another school teacher by the name of Minne Freeman led her students to safety. Miss Freeman became a real heroine. All the people of Nebraska knew about the brave young lady who led her children to safety through the terrible blizzard.

In the fall of the year prairie fires were a great problem. The dry prairie grass caught fire easily. A prairie fire would burn for many, many miles.

Settlers plowed "fire guards" around their houses and barns. These strips of plowed ground turned aside the prairie fires.

But every year prairie fires roared over the land. Houses, barns and haystacks went up in smoke. Even worse, people would be caught in the flames and killed.

Pioneer parents warned their children to watch for prairie fires. If the children saw smoke rising in the sky, they were to run for home as fast as they could.

During the summers of 1874 and 1875 the prairie pioneers faced another problem — grasshoppers!

This is how it happened.

A family of pioneers is sitting around the dinner table. Suddenly, they notice that it has become very dark. Father says, "Looks as though a storm is coming up."

They walk outside to watch the storm. But the clouds do not look like the usual storm clouds.

"Pa, what kind of clouds are those?" asks Mother.

Before he can answer, grasshoppers start falling from the sky. There are billions and billions of the insects. They begin to eat every green plant in sight.

Father yells, "Hurry, everybody. Get your brooms and rakes. I'll start a fire, and we'll try to burn up these terrible grasshoppers!"

But nothing could stop the grasshoppers. There were too many to be burned. A farmer in Butler County tried something else. He covered his garden plants with blankets. And the grasshoppers ate both the blankets and the plants!

The grasshoppers covered the railroad tracks. The trains could not run. The tracks were too slippery.

The grasshoppers wiped out many pioneer farmers. One pioneer in Kearney County traded his 320 acre farm for a horse. He hitched the horse to a wagon and took his family back to Illinois — away from the terrible grasshoppers.

But there were many people who did not leave the land. People from the eastern states collected food and clothing for the settlers.

One big box of clothing arrived in York. The settlers were very happy. Most of them really needed some new clothing.

They opened the box and began to unpack the clothing. What a surprise they had! The box was filled with ladies' party dresses and men's fancy clothes.

The settlers were sad and disappointed. They couldn't use that kind of clothing. Then someone had an idea.

"Why not dress up in those fancy clothes," he said, "and then we can have a party?"

So that is what the pioneers of York County did. They had a good time and for a short while forgot about the grasshoppers.

"It was during these hard years of the grasshoppers that pioneer Nebraskans became known as bugeaters. Remember?"

While life was sometimes hard, the prairie pioneers had many good times.

Pioneer children enjoyed going to school. Of course, the school houses, out in the country, were not always the best. Families would get together and build a school of logs.

In Seward County children had trouble doing their lessons. The wind blew in between the logs in the wall and scattered books and papers all over the ground.

In Fillmore County a pioneer family with several children lived several miles from the school house.

The father was afraid his children would get lost on the prairie. So he plowed a furrow from the house to the school. His children walked along the furrow to school every day.

There was one problem! On warm days rattlesnakes liked to crawl onto the dirt and sun themselves. The children had to watch carefully where they walked.

In many parts of Nebraska schools were made of sod. Can you see the teacher in this picture?

The teachers were usually young men or women. None of them had gone to college. Most of them had only attended grade school.

But these pioneer teachers worked hard. They wanted their students to learn their three "r's" — reading, 'riting and 'rithmetic. And they also knew that they could mix "licking" with "learning."

The country school house was always busy. They were used day and night, every day of the week.

Church services were conducted in the school houses on Sunday. Saturday night there would be a spelling bee or a box social And at least once a week there would be a dance in the school house.

In York County two brothers wanted to go to a dance. They were short of money and could buy only one pair of shoes.

So, they walked bare footed to the school house carrying the one pair of shoes. Then, when they reached the school, one brother put on the shoes, went inside and danced with the pretty girls.

The other brother waited outside for his turn to put on the shoes and join in the dancing.

As the years passed pioneer farmers moved farther and farther west across Nebraska.

Since there was less rainfall in western Nebraska, these pioneers had to learn new ways of farming the dry land.

In time they began to irrigate their crops. With irrigation, the western land produced fine crops.

But most of western Nebraska remained the home of the cowboys and cattle.

"I want to remind you of some important things about Nebraska's prairie pioneers. First of all, the pioneers planted thousands of trees on the prairie. They wanted to see trees growing on the barren prairie. They knew that in time the trees could be cut down for firewood. And they also hoped that the trees would bring more rainfall."

"Second, I want you to remember that the windmill is a fine monument to our pioneer farmers. The windmill pumped water for the pioneers and their livestock. The windmill helped the prairie pioneers live on the land."

The cottonwood is Nebraska's State Tree.

Picture Power

Look carefully at this photograph. What do you see?

Everyone will see the cow on the roof. Did you notice that the boys are all barefoot? What about the watermelon? This picture was taken to be sent to relatives in the East. The watermelon, about twice as big as any grown back in the East, showed that Nebraska was a very fertile country.

Notice the table on which the watermelon sits. Don't you suppose the mother brought this table with her to Nebraska from her old home in the East? And notice the fine tablecloth.

Chapter 21:
Cowpunchers and Longhorns

As you know, huge herds of buffalo once roamed the hills, valleys and prairies of western Nebraska.

You also know that the Indians hunted the buffalo for food. The buffalo was the Indians' supermarket. Just about everything the Indian needed for food and clothing came from the buffalo.

The covered wagon pioneers were always excited when they saw their first buffalo. The men in the wagon trains hunted the buffalo. But these pioneers did not kill many of the animals. There were still thousands and thousands of buffalo left for the Indians.

Then the railroads came into buffalo country. The trains brought white hunters who owned high-powered rifles. These men began to hunt the buffalo.

What did these white hunters take from the buffalo they killed?

This photograph will give you the answer:

First, notice the pieces of meat hanging from the wooden rack. Those are buffalo tongues.

Now look on the ground. There you see buffalo hides, or robes, stretched out to dry.

The hide and the tongue — those are the only two parts of the buffalo the hunters wanted. The hides and tongues were then taken to a nearby railroad depot, where they were shipped east.

The white hunters killed thousands of buffalo every month. The herds grew smaller and smaller. And, of course, the Indians became very angry. They hated the white hunters who were slaughtering the buffalo.

The killing of the buffalo, more than any other thing, caused the Indians of the plains to go on the warpath. They decided to fight to keep the white hunters and the white settlers from taking their hunting grounds.

The war between the whites and the Indians went on for many years. It was a terrible war. Finally the Indians were forced to surrender.

The government said that the defeated Indians must get out of the way of the white settlers. The Indians must live on "reservations." White men, known as agents, were sent to watch over the Indians. The agents made certain that the Indians stayed on the reservation.

Since the Indians could no longer hunt buffalo, the government agreed to feed them.

The Indians were not happy on the reservations. For years they had traveled freely over the beautiful prairies. Now they had to stay in one place. And it was not a very good place at that. The Indian reservations were usually laid out in poor country.

The Army built forts near the reservations. Fort Robinson, in northwestern Nebraska, was built near the Indian reservations. Soldiers from Fort Robinson were involved in the wars involving the plains Indians.

At Fort Robinson one of the great Indian war leaders, Crazy Horse, was killed after he surrendered.

Fort Niobrara, in Cherry County, was another Army fort built to guard the reservations.

Now we must look at what was happening in Texas, a state far south of Nebraska.

Down in Texas there were ranchers who owned thousands of longhorn cattle. But the ranchers could not find anyone to buy their longhorns.

Then railroads began to reach west across the Kansas and Nebraska plains. The Texas cattlemen had an idea. They would drive their cattle north to these railroads. Men who wanted to buy the long-horns would meet the Texas cattlemen at towns along the railroads.

It was a great idea! The Texas ranchers would sell their cattle and make money. And the buyers would have the cattle they needed.

Government agents wanted to buy longhorns for the hungry reservation Indians. Eastern meat companies wanted cattle to be killed and made into meat. Other cattle would be bought by Kansas and Nebraska ranchers who wanted cattle for their ranches.

The Texas ranchers rounded up a herd of two or three thousand longhorns. They hired men to drive the herd north to the railroad cowtowns.

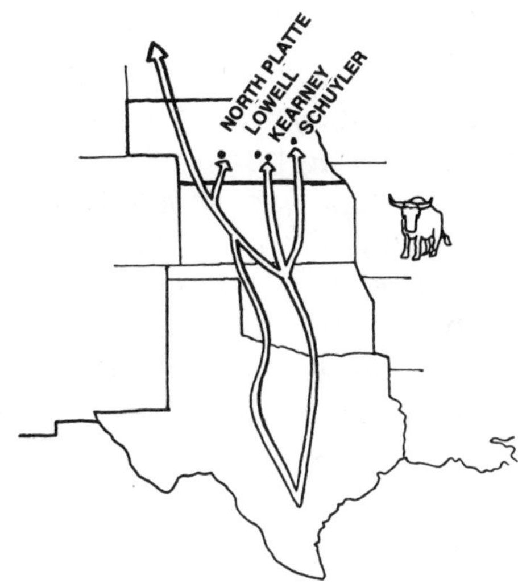

These trail hands, as they were called, were usually young fellows. Some of them were no more than fifteen years old.

An experienced cowboy would be made the trail boss. There would be ten or twelve other cowboys in the crew. One of the men, known as the wrangler, spent all his time caring for the horses.

The trail boss and the other cowboys rode with the herd all day. The cowboys with the least experience rode behind the herd. The dust was terrible behind the herd. Riding "drag," as it was called, was the worst job a cowboy could have.

Late in the evening the cattle were stopped and the cowboys let them settle down for the night.

All night the cowboys took turns riding around the herd. The cowboys usually sang softly, the music keeping the cattle quiet.

The trail hands soon learned to get along without much sleep. The boss told them they could catch up on their sleep when they got to Nebraska!

A very important member of the trail crew was the cook. In his chuck wagon, the cook carried all the things he needed to prepare meals for the men.

One thing for sure: the cowboys never argued with the cook. The cook was king of the camp.

The trip from Texas to one of the cow towns might take as long as three months. The longhorns could travel about twenty miles a day. But there were always delays.

In dry weather the thirsty cattle did not move very fast. The herd might be driven far from the trail in order to find water.

Then, the cattle might stampede. Stampedes might come at any time, day or night. One minute the cattle would be behaving just fine. Next minute the whole herd would be off and running.

It could take the trail hands several days to round up the cattle. During a stampede the cattle might run five or ten miles. They would be scattered in every direction.

They also lost time at the river crossings. Western rivers were usually in flood in the spring when the herds went north. And the longhorns had to be forced into swimming the deep, muddy rivers. The cowboys rode their horses right into the river, too. They had to make the longhorns swim across and climb out of the river on dry ground.

Crossing a river was the most dangerous part of the trail hands' work. Many men died at the river crossings.

After months on the trail, the herd of longhorns came to the end of the trail. Up ahead lay the railroad and the little cowtown.

The trail boss met with cattle buyers. A deal for the cattle was made. Then the boss returned to the camp and paid off the trail hands.

The boys were really happy now. With their coins jingling in their pockets, they headed for town.

Most of the cowboys went to the stores in town and bought the supplies they needed for the coming year.

But there were always a few of the cowboys who didn't have good sense. They went right to the saloons and gambling houses and in a few hours spent all their money.

Now let's talk about the cattle trails and cowtowns of Nebraska.

In the 1860's herds of Texas longhorns showed up at Brownville and Nebraska. After swimming the Missouri River, the longhorns were driven on to Illinois.

About ten years later many herds came to Schuyler which lay on the Union Pacific Railroad. Schuyler was probably the first important cowtown in Nebraska.

The farmers who lived south of Schuyler, however, did not like having the Texas longhorns cross their land. The Texas cattle trampled crops and tore down fences. But more important, these cattle left behind a terrible disease, known as Texas fever, which killed off all the farmers' cattle.

So the Butler County farmers closed the trail. With rifles and shotguns in hand, they met the Texas cowboys. They told the Texans to take their cattle some other place.

So, in order to get away from the angry farmers, the Texas cowboys moved their trail farther west.

Lowell and Kearney then became shipping points for the Texas cattle. Both towns were known as wide-open cowtowns.

The citizens of Kearney, however, grew tired of having the Texas cowboys shoot up their town. They ordered the cowboys to leave. There were fights between the townspeople and the cowboys. Finally, the cowboys pulled out. They began to drive their cattle to Plum Creek (which is now Lexington) and North Platte.

The best known, and probably the most important, cowtown in Nebraska was Ogallala. For many years this was the end of the trail for the Texas herds. During the early summer the South Platte River valley around Ogallala was filled with thousands of longhorns waiting to be sold.

Andy Adams was a Texas cowboy who visited Ogallala at this time. He said that Ogallala had thirty saloons, but not one church. He said Ogallala was just about the roughest town along the cattle trail.

Ogallala was a rough town. During the summer Texas cowboys filled the streets of town. They spent their money freely in Ogallala's saloons and gambling houses. And like every cowtown, Ogallala had a cemetery known as Boot Hill. Here is where the fellows, killed in fights, were buried. Most of them still had their "boots on" when they were buried.

For about twenty years herds of Texas cattle came up the trail into Nebraska. Then railroads were built to Texas, and it no longer paid to drive the cattle over the trails.

And the longhorn began to disappear, too. The long-legged, tough longhorn was just the animal to be used on the trail. But it was not a very good meat animal. Cattlemen began to raise other breeds of cattle. These new breeds had a lot more meat on their bones than did the old longhorn.

The prairies of western Nebraska were now open for the cattle ranchers. The buffalo and the Indians were gone. It looked as though cattle ranchers could make a lot of money.

In the first place, Texas longhorns were very cheap. And there was so much land available that none of the pioneer ranchers bothered to buy land. They just turned their longhorns out on the free grass. After the longhorns had fattened up, the ranchers took them to market and sold them — at a nice profit.

These were the days of the open range — when ranchers ran their cattle on land where there were no fences.

Soon, however, the days of the open range came to an end. There were too many cattle on the prairie. The price of cattle dropped.

Then came terrible winter blizzards. The snow and ice buried the grass. Water holes were frozen solid. Thousands of cattle died. Many ranchers lost everything they had. And the prairies of western Nebraska were covered with the bones of dead cattle.

There were some pioneer ranchers who were willing to start again. This time, however, they got their own land. And they strung barbed wire fences around their pastures.

They bought new breeds of cattle. Angus, Shorthorn and Hereford cattle replaced the Texas longhorns. The new cattle needed more care and attention than the longhorns; but they produced more beef. They made more money for their owners.

The cattle industry in Nebraska changed in just a few years. The days of the open range were gone. Ranches began to appear on the prairies and in the Sand Hills.

The cowboys, however, were still around. And what interesting fellows they were!

Most of the cowboys were young men. As a rule they didn't talk much about themselves. Most of the Nebraska cowboys probably came from farms. But there were others who came from eastern cities. Some were well-educated.

You could always tell a cowboy by his clothing. He wore a tall, broad-brimmed hat, that kept the sun from blistering his face. The big hat also made a good bucket for carrying water to his horse.

A handkerchief around the neck was used to cover his face and nose. It kept the choking dust out of his throat.

High-heeled boots kept his foot in the stirrup. But the heel was shaped so that it would slip easily out of the stirrup in case the cowboy fell out of the saddle.

One thing every cowboy feared— being "hung up." That is, having a foot caught in the stirrup and being dragged by a runaway horse.

Don't think that cowboys never were thrown from their horses. As an old cowboy once said, "There never was a horse that couldn't be rode, and a cowboy who couldn't be throwed!"

Of course, you couldn't be a cowboy without a horse. One reason so many cowboys wore high-heeled boots was so they could not walk.

There is the story of one Nebraska rancher who always kept a saddled horse right outside his house. When he had to go to the barn, which was just a hundred feet away, he rode the horse.

A man asked him why he rode the horse instead of walking. The rancher said, "If God had wanted men to walk, He would have given them four feet!"

The cowboy took good care of his horses. Only in an emergency would the cowboy gallop his horse. I'm sure old-time cowboys are really mad when they watch our TV cowboys gallop their horses all the time. No real cowboy would wear out a good horse that way.

The same thing is true with six-shooters. Old time cowboys seldom wore guns when they worked. They just got in the

way. A few would strap on pistols when they went into town. But then the guns were more for show than anything else.

What about spurs? On many Nebraska ranches cowboys were not permitted to wear spurs. One Nebraska rancher said that good cowboys did not need spurs. Only those who didn't know how to handle horses wore spurs.

So, the Texas cowboys brought their longhorns up the trail to Nebraska. Many of the Texas cowboys went to work for Nebraska ranchers. There were many young men from Nebraska's towns and farms who wanted to become cowboys.

These young men soon learned that "punching" cattle was not easy. The cowpunchers worked long hours and didn't get very good pay.

But these cowpunchers were important Nebraska pioneers. In western Nebraska, as you "listen to the land," you can hear the story of the cowpunchers and longhorns.

Cattle Brands

Cattlemen put brands on the cattle they owned. These brands were applied with a hot branding iron.
The hot iron burned away the hair and left the brand.

Cowboys had to learn to "read" these brands. If they found some cattle out on the prairie, the brand on the cattle would tell them who the animals belonged to.

Here are some cattle brands. See if you can "read" them:

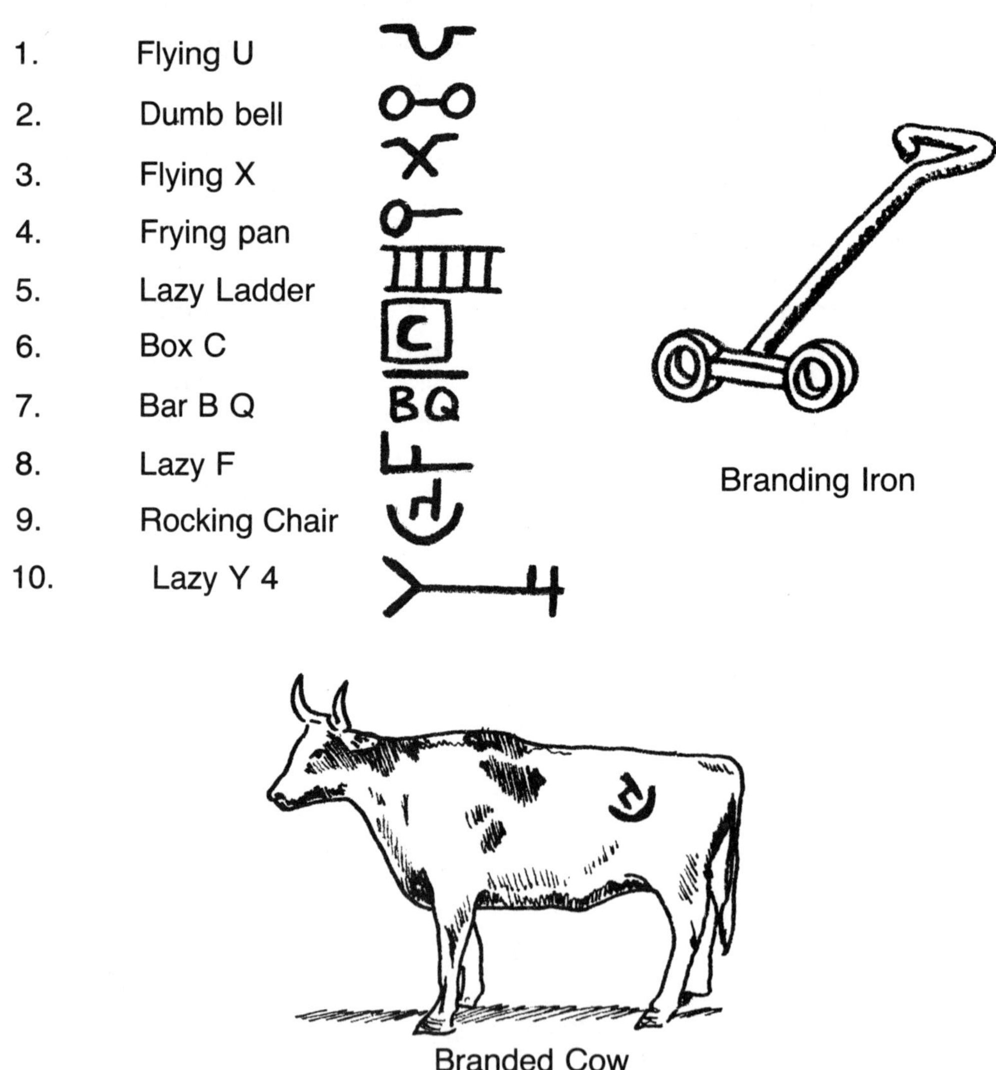

Branding Iron

Branded Cow

Chapter 22:
From Many Lands

"I want to ask you a very important question. Where did Nebraska's pioneers come from?

"The stories in this chapter will help you answer this question."

Nebraska's pioneers came from many different places. Some of our pioneers came from eastern states, such as Pennsylvania, New York and Illinois.

These pioneers at first came to Nebraska by covered wagon. Later they could come up the Missouri River on steamboats. Finally, they made the long journey by railroad trains.

Other pioneers came to Nebraska from lands across the Atlantic and Pacific Oceans.

They came from Germany, Sweden, Ireland and other European countries. They came from Mexico and South America. They also came from Africa and Asia.

"Yes, Nebraska's pioneers came from many lands."

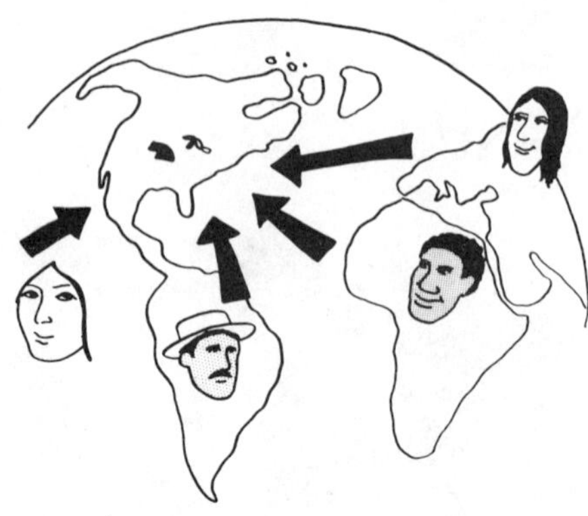

To people in these foreign lands, Nebraska offered a future. People could own their own land in Nebraska. They could open their own businesses. Their children could go to school. And they were free to attend any church. There were many opportunities in Nebraska. And there was freedom in Nebraska.

Many people in Europe and other foreign lands were not free. Poor people could not own land. The people paid high taxes. Many could not vote. Worst of all, there were many wars in Europe. Every young man had to serve years in the army.

"So, you see, our ancestors, who lived in foreign lands, had many reasons for wanting to come to America."

"I have another question for you. How did these people who lived in other lands hear about Nebraska?"

The people who lived in foreign lands received letters from friends and relatives who had come to Nebraska.

These letters told them about Nebraska. They told them about the land and about the freedom they enjoyed in our State.

The letters told the people to think about coming to Nebraska. They wouldn't be sorry. Nebraska was a fine country.

Newspapers also helped people in other lands find out about Nebraska. Many Nebraska newspapers were printed in foreign languages. These newspapers were sent all over the world.

People read about Nebraska farms and Nebraska towns. They read about all the good things that were happening in this new land.

Many little books, or pamphlets, were written about Nebraska. Some of the pamphlets were published by the State of Nebraska. Others were written by town companies and railroads.

All of these pamphlets had one purpose. They wanted to tell people about Nebraska.

The railroad companies were really interested in bringing people here. Look at this photograph:

This railroad car brought people to visit Crete and Saline County.

The car was owned by the Burlington Railroad. Persons who wanted to visit Saline County could ride in this car to Nebraska. The cost of riding in this special car was very reasonable.

So people from the East and people from foreign lands came to look at Saline County. The people of Saline County hoped some of these visitors would decide to settle in their county.

Like every county in Nebraska, Saline County needed pioneers.

Speaking of Saline County, look at this land poster put out by the Burlington Railroad.

Is there anything unusual about this poster?

Yes, it is written in a foreign language. It is written in the Czech language.

The Burlington Railroad sent this poster to Czech communities in the eastern United States. Some of the posters may have been sent to Europe.

The poster tells the Czechs about the fine land available in Saline County. According to the drawings, in just six years a pioneer could build up a fine farm on this rich land.

This marker, between Wilber and Crete, tells the story of the Czech pioneers who settled here.

Perhaps some of these Czech pioneers came to Saline County after reading the poster.

The railroads hired men to go to foreign countries to tell people about Nebraska.

These men, who were called agents, usually were natives of the country they visited. The men went to the villages where they had lived before they came to Nebraska.

The agents would talk to the people. They would tell them about Nebraska. There would usually be some people who wanted to come to Nebraska.

The agents would then bring the people to America. They would buy the railroad and steamship tickets. Usually, the agents would travel with the people. They did all they could to help them.

There was a great deal of competition between the agents of the different railroads. A group of immigrants, for example, might be on their way to Nebraska. Agents from the Kansas railroads would talk with them. They would try to get the people to change their minds and come to Kansas.

Finally the immigrants would arrive in Lincoln. The women and children would stay in this building while the men went to look for land or for jobs. The building was known as The Emigrant House.

Many of our immigrant ancestors did not come directly to Nebraska.

They stopped for a time in cities such as Chicago, Illlinois, and Milwaukee, Wisconsin.

In these large cities the men (and often the women) found jobs. They saved their money. Then they would come to Nebraska with enough money to buy a farm or to start a business.

For example, a group of Danish immigrants lived in Milwaukee. They organized a club they called the Danish Land and Homestead Colony. They held meetings and talked about moving to Nebraska.

Several men were sent to look for a good place for the Danish people to settle in Nebraska. They reported back to Milwaukee that they had found a good place.

The Danish immigrants moved to Nebraska and founded the town of Dannebrog in Howard County.

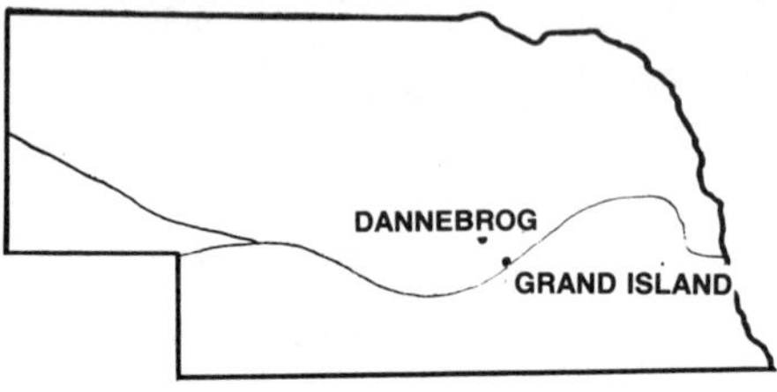

Another group of immigrants built the town of Grand Island. These were German immigrants who lived in Davenport, Iowa.

The Germans formed a town company. They decided to build their town in the Platte Valley of Nebraska.

Why did they choose the Platte Valley? Because they believed that a railroad one day would be built through the Platte Valley. And they also believed that the capital of the United States might be moved to Nebraska.

So in 1857 these German pioneers drove their oxen and wagons across Iowa. They started up the Platte Valley.

After several weeks of hard travel, the Germans stopped their wagons. They came to the spot where they wanted to build their town. They named the town Grand Island.

The German pioneers built log cabins in which to live. Some of them plowed the sod and planted crops. Others opened stores along the trail. They traded with the pioneers who were going west on the trail.

In 1866 the Union Pacific Railroad came to Grand Island. A new town grew up around the depot. Grand Island became an important and prosperous town.

The German pioneers were proud to have built this city.

O.K. Store which was built by Mr. Wiebe and Mr. Koenig, two of the German pioneers.

Wyoming House was one of Grand Island's hotels. Notice that the sign just above the porch is in German.

While many immigrant pioneers built towns, others wanted to farm. Many immigrant families settled on the land.

These immigrants wanted to live among their own people. It is easy to understand how they felt. They wanted people for neighbors who spoke their language and who shared their customs.

So, in many Nebraska counties there were immigrant groups who settled in close groups.

Here for example is a map of Kearney County which shows where the different immigrants settled:

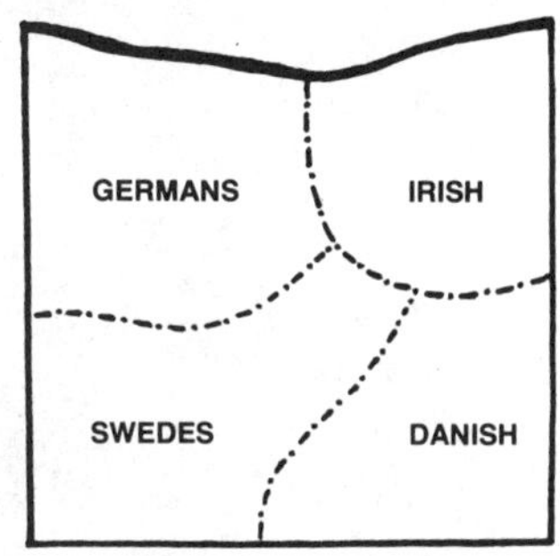

These are the immigrant groups which settled in Dodge County.

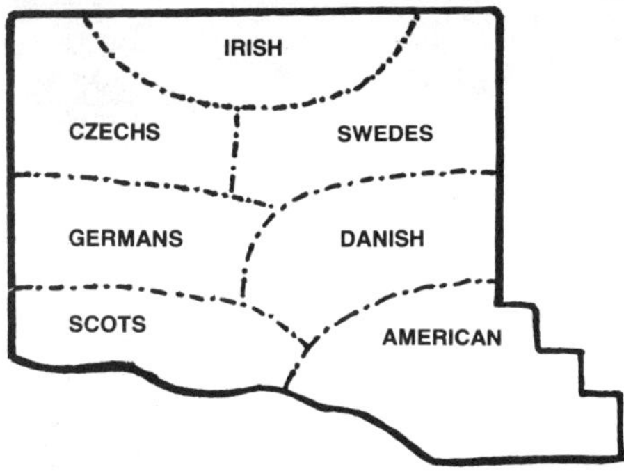

A church was often the center of these immigrant farm communities. The services in these churches were usually in foreign languages.

The center of many Czech communities was the lodge. Here the people met for dances and for other social events. The lodge hall was an important meeting place for these immigrant people.

It is important for us to remember that these immigrants continued to speak the language of the country from which they came.

Newspapers in many Nebraska towns were printed in foreign languages. Church services were held in foreign languages; and even some schools were taught in foreign languages. If you walked down the main street of some Nebraska towns, you would not hear a word of English — only the foreign language of the immigrants who lived in the town.

It was very hard for the immigrants to give up their languages and customs. They wanted to keep the customs of their homelands.

But little by little the immigrants and their children began to forget about the land from which they came. They tried hard to become Americans.

While we are proud to be citizens of the United States, we should also be proud of our immigrant ancestors.

After all, these brave people left their far away homes and came to America. And they came so that we might enjoy the freedom of America. They came so that we might have a future.

"The story of Nebraska includes the story of the people who came from many lands to build our State. These immigrant people were important pioneers. They prepared the way for us!"

Heritage Special

Black Nebraskans were important pioneers.

There were Black Pioneers who homesteaded in Nebraska.

And there were many Black cowboys in Nebraska. This man worked on a ranch in Kimball County.

Yes, there were Black Nebraskans who helped build our towns and make our farms and ranches.

There were Black men who served in the United States Army.

Black Nebraskans share in every part of our Nebraska Heritage!

Our Pioneer Heritage

"I know that you have learned some very important things. First, you have learned that history is the story of people.

"And you have learned that history is all around you in Nebraska."

"Yes, and you've learned about some very interesting and important people — Nebraska's pioneers."

Nebraska has had many different kinds of pioneers.

There were the prairie pioneers who laid out our towns and built our farms and ranches.

There were the covered wagon pioneers and the political pioneers. There were the soldiers and cowpunchers.

Nebraska's pioneers came from many lands. Pioneer men and women were of many races and cultures. Black pioneers, Mexican pioneers, pioneers who came from all over the world made history in Nebraska.

And we must not forget the Indians, who were here in Nebraska when the pioneers arrived. These Indians are important people in Nebraska's heritage, too.

"I know you have been thinking about the pioneers in your very own families."

First of all, your great grandparents who decided to come to America. How brave they were! They knew that in America there would be freedom and opportunity.

And there were many other pioneers in your family. Perhaps your grandmother who decided to be a teacher, a doctor or a lawyer.

There was probably a grandfather who decided that his future lay in Nebraska. So he took the long trip by covered wagon or steam train to the place called Nebraska. He built a house for his family, and then broke the sod. He planted his crops and looked forward to the future harvests of his rich land.

And remember: there are pioneers in every generation.

Not many years ago there were automobile pioneers in Nebraska. Men like Mr. Hove in Minden who built his own automobile.

Folks in town laughed at him, but Mr. Hove knew that the automobile was important. He knew that the auto would replace the horse and buggy.

And there were our pioneer farmers. Perhaps your grandfather was one of the first to use a tractor. Many of his neighbors said that horses were better than tractors. But he went ahead and bought a tractor anyway.

There were family pioneers who opened new businesses in town. They realized that there was a need for new businesses. And they helped their friends see the opportunities for the future.

And perhaps most important, in every generation there were future pioneers who went to school. Your grand-parents, your parents and all your relatives went to school to prepare for the future.

"So, what kind of pioneer do you want to be?

"What do you want to do to prepare the way for the next generation of Nebraskans?"

Now, you are going to use your imagination. You are visiting a Nebraska school. The year is 2015.

The school is certainly different from the school you went to, back in the 1980's.

Listen to the teacher talk to the class: "Children, today we are going to talk about Nebraska's pioneers. Do any of you have some stories about your families' pioneers?"

Hands fly up all over the room. The teacher calls on one girl.

"I would like to tell you about my father. He helped make a new kind of fuel for our automobiles."

Another student speaks: "And I'd like you to know about my uncle who learned how to raise new crops in Nebraska."

A third student also wants to talk: "I'll bet all of you have heard of my mother. She opened a business in town — the first of its kind in Nebraska."

"Do you know who these students are talking about?
"Yes, they are talking about you. Those are your children sitting in the classroom. And they know that they are a part of history."

"Please take some time to think about your future. You will see that there are many things you and your friends can do. You can help prepare the way for your children."
"You can be pioneers!"

Operation Attic

Many years ago houses had a place called an attic.

This was the room under the roof. It was the place where trunks and boxes of old things were stored.

The attic was a wonderful place for children to play. As they looked through boxes and trunks they found things that belonged to their parents and their grandparents.

The attic helped them learn about their heritage.

Do you know what? You need to have an attic of your own. Why? Because twenty-five or thirty years from now your children will be asking you questions:

"Dad, what were you doing when you were my age?"

"Mom, what was school like back then?"

"What did you do for fun?"

"What did our town look like?"

"How did you farm back in those days?"

Yes, your children will have many, many questions. And it is important for you to have answers for their questions.

So, why don't you do this. Take a large envelope. On the outside of the envelope write these words:

"TO MY CHILDREN. TO BE OPENED IN THE YEAR 2015 A.D."

Now you must decide what things you want to save for your children to see when they open the envelope.

What kinds of things do you think they would like to have that tell about you?

For sure they would like to see pictures of you and your friends. I'll bet they would also like to see pictures of your school and your home.

I know one thing that would be exciting for your children: if they could hear your voice.

Look back in Chapter Five. Find the list of questions that you asked your parents. Turn on your tape recorder and *you* answer those questions. I know your children will really like hearing you talk about yourself.

Now if you are too shy to use the tape recorder, write down the answers. Your children will enjoy reading what you have to say.

The photographs, tape cassettes and written stories your children find in your attic will help them understand that they are a part of history.

And what fun they will have hearing about how you went to school "back in the good, old days."

I hope you have enjoyed learning about our pioneer heritage. And I hope you go right on learning about Nebraska.

Listen to the stories your parents and grandparents have to tell you. Look around where you live. Keep on looking and listening for your heritage.

Your friend,

Robert Manley

Dr. Robert Manley

"Best of luck to all you pioneers of the future!"

Photo Credits

NSHS — Nebraska State Historical Society
NG&P — Nebraska Game & Parks Commission
KSHS — Kansas State Historical Society

Page IV	NSHS
3	NSHS
5	NSHS
20	"Barber Shop" — Roland Kelley, Rising City, NE All others — NSHS
21	NSHS
22	NSHS
40	Solomon D. Butcher Collection, NSHS
48	NG&P
50	NSHS
54	NG&P
58	NSHS
61	Smithsonian Institution, National Anthropological Archives, Bureau of American Ethnology Collection
65	NSHS
76	NSHS
77	NSHS
79	NG&P
94	NSHS
96	NSHS
97	NSHS
104	Kansas City, MO — Public Library
105	NSHS
106	NSHS
112	NSHS
115	NSHS
116	NSHS
118	NSHS
120	Poster — NSHS "Statesman" — Solomon D. Butcher Collection — NSHS
121	All — NSHS
122	Coal Mine — Brownville Historical Society Others: West Point, NE Library
123	"Parade" — Stuhr Museum, Grand Island, NE "Baseball Team" — Dodge Co., NE Historical Society Others — NSHS
124	Upper Left — Stuhr Museum Lower Left — Otoe Co., NE Museum All Others — NSHS
125	School Building — Exterior — West Point, NE Public Library All Others — NSHS
129	NSHS
130	NSHS
131	NSHS
132	Middle picture — Rt. Hand Column — Omaha Public Library All Others — NSHS
134	Courthouse — Roger Sikes Joel Hull — NSHS
135	NSHS
136	Stuhr Museum
137	"Capitol" — NG&P Others — NSHS
138	NSHS

139 Left — Harris & Ewing
Right — NSHS
141 NSHS
142 NSHS
143 NSHS
144 Top — NSHS
Bottom — Union Pacific Railroad Museum Collection
145 NSHS
146 NSHS
147 Stuhr Museum
148 NSHS
150 NSHS
151 NSHS
152 NSHS
153 NSHS
154 NSHS
155 NSHS
158 NSHS
159 NSHS
161 Lower Left — Kansas State Historical Society
Upper right — NG&P
162 NSHS
163 Solomon D. Butcher Collection, NSHS
165 NSHS
166 NSHS
168 NSHS
169 NSHS
170 Solomon D. Butcher Collection, NSHS
171 Buffalo — NG&P
Other — University of Oklahoma
172 Left column — KSHS
Right column — NSHS
173 KSHS
174 KSHS
175 NSHS
177 NSHS
178 NSHS
179 NSHS
181 NSHS
183 NSHS
184 NSHS
185 NSHS
186 NSHS
188 Mrs. M. Wox
189 NSHS
192 Top of Page — Andy Hove
Others — NSHS
193 NSHS